BUILDING PEOPLE

SUNDAY EMAILS
FROM A CEO

BUILDING PEOPLE

SUNDAY EMAILS
FROM A CEO

LIEW MUN LEONG

WILEY

John Wiley & Sons (Asia) Pte Ltd

Other Wiley Editorial Offices

John Wiley & Sons, 111 River Street, Hoboken, NJ 07030, US
John Wiley & Sons, The Atrium Southern Gate, Chichester PO19 8SQ, England
John Wiley & Sons (Canada) Ltd., 5353 Dundas Street West, Suite 400, Toronto Ontario M9B 6HB, Canada
John Wiley & Sons Australia Ltd., 42 McDougall Street, Milton, Queensland 4064, Australia
Wiley-VCH, Boschstrasse 12, D-69469 Weinheim, Germany

Library of Congress Cataloging-in-Publication Data

ISBN 978-0470-822906

Typeset in 11/14 Points Rotis Serif by JC Ruxpin Pte. Ltd.
Printed in Singapore by Markono Print Media Pte. Ltd.
10 9 8 7 6 5 4 3 2 1

TABLE OF CONTENTS

Chapter 3   61
Day-to-Day Business — Success is in the Details

Chapter 4   93
Learning Journeys

FOREWORD

Choices and Decisions

When I was looking around in 1996 for a CEO to lead Pidemco Land,[1] Liew Mun Leong came to mind.

I first had the opportunity to observe Mun Leong at work when he was CEO[2] of the Singapore Institute of Standards and Industrial Research (SISIR). He was focused, and very particular in trying to understand what made sense. He was always thinking and looking for ways to make improvements, whether in terms of the people and systems in the institution or in reaching out to the international communities such as the International Standards Organisation. This enabled SISIR to punch above its weight and make a meaningful contribution to the community in various ways. He strongly promoted the use of the ISO9000 platform as the foundation for process improvements in Singapore, not just for the manufacturing industry but also in pioneering this framework for the service industries as well as for the smaller companies. Much of these groundbreaking successes were driven by Mun Leong's refusal to take no for an answer, and his rejection of convention as a lame reason for not trying to push the boundaries of the possible.

But what struck me most was, and still is, his interest in people. Mun Leong is tireless in looking out for young people, as well as in teasing out the best in all sorts of people, including older as well as less-educated people. He is always giving people an opportunity or a second chance to test themselves and to grow.

He is also a practical and down-to-earth man. While not a learned man in the classical sense, he has a very strong set of values and principles. His father had given him much of his rootedness and resilience in attitudes. Mun Leong often quotes his father's many Cantonese homilies, which obviously shaped his own thinking and value system. However busy he is, he never fails to bring home for his mother her favourite roast goose from Hong Kong whenever he returns from his travel there. He is a filial son, and also a conscientious father.

He has his failings and blind spots of course, like all of us. But stubbornness and determination are two sides of the same coin.

Mun Leong would make a good CEO for Pidemco if we were to reposition and shape it as a new model real estate company, one that is professional, innovative, resourceful and would last beyond the tenure of a typical founder-owner of real estate companies we find in Asia. Mun Leong has the interest and tenacity to build a team. He has the instincts and deep commitment to build a lasting institution in a newly emerging Asia. The bonus was that he knew the construction and property development industry from ground up, so to speak, being a meticulous civil engineer who had been involved in many projects, including the building of the award-winning Changi airport.

It was a happy choice for Pidemco when Mun Leong accepted the challenge of running and transforming a collection of "third-class buildings in first-class locations", as one pundit described Pidemco.

It was yet again another difficult choice in 2000.

There had been strong market rumours that DBS was divesting its non-core property arm DBS Land. With support from its Pidemco team, Singapore Technologies decided to make an unsolicited bid. Little did we know that DBS was already in the midst of negotiating the terms for a sale to an international bidder.[3] The international bidder decided not to match the unsolicited offer. This paved the way for Pidemco Land and DBS Land to form CapitaLand.

With this came the difficult decision of choosing a CEO. Both companies had strong, competent CEOs. It was clear that it should be the best man for the job, but best man in what context?

In the end, Mun Leong was chosen to head CapitaLand, with an eye to a different future. Mun Leong would have an edge if the newly merged company were to be built as a professionally managed real estate institution, with highly competent and committed teams that can develop new ideas, services and products, and with the potential to scale up as a global company.

Almost immediately after shareholders had approved the merger, CapitaLand ran right into a perfect storm. The internet bubble burst in 2000, followed by the 9/11 attacks in the US in 2001, the Bali bombings in 2002, and SARS and the Iraq war in 2003. Singapore also experienced one of its worst economic crises in 2001, while the region was still struggling to emerge from the 1997 Asian financial crisis.

Under Mun Leong's leadership, CapitaLand has overcome these odds and much doubt to become one of the most progressive and innovative real estate companies in Asia. It has successfully pioneered the S-REIT[4] market in Singapore, after six long years of tireless perseverance. It helped Hong Kong launch its landmark Link REIT. It has also become one of the largest private equity real estate fund managers in Asia.

Through these ups and downs, Mun Leong continued his prototype "blog" conversations with his staff, mostly written on Sundays, and sometimes written during his long plane journeys home. Started in 1998, Mun Leong regularly shares his observations, thoughts, ideas, joys and disappointments with all his staff and board members. His candid Sunday weekly musings tell of his passions and enthusiasms, his travels and the people he has met. His experiences, anecdotes, or frank opinions would either spur fresh ideas, raise new questions or become a refreshing challenge to his CapitaLand team to push the envelope. More importantly, he shares openly on his work ethics and philosophies on various aspects of life, continuing his natural instincts to be coach, mentor, brother and friend to his colleagues. Through these Sunday blog-style emails, he continues to imbue CapitaLanders with his perfectionist and paranoid commitment to excellence, and his "never-give-up" and "can-do" spirit.

The journey is not over, of course. There are many more mountains to climb and rivers to cross in a now booming and thriving Asia that is increasingly interconnected to the world. Mun Leong continues to build for the future. He passionately believes in the linking between building for people and building people. His latest initiative is the CapitaLand Institute of Management and Business, or CLIMB, to focus on the training and development of the next generation of leaders and managers for CapitaLand. This collection of his Sunday email messages is also intended to facilitate sharing with his colleagues in the CLIMB courses.

I was privileged to have been copied on many of Mun Leong's Sunday emails. I enjoyed them, and welcome you to share and enjoy this selection of nuggets as you continue to make choices and decisions as a fellow traveller in life.

Ho Ching
Executive Director and CEO
Temasek Holdings

End Notes

1 Temasek transferred Pidemco Land to Singapore Technologies at peak market valuation in 1996, with the remit of bringing in new leadership and eventually listing it.
2 Mun Leong was CEO of SISIR from 1988 to 1992, when he was headhunted to run listed construction company, L&M.
3 Little did we know that neither Pidemco nor Singapore Technologies were considered for the invitation to bid for DBS Land.
4 Singapore Real Estate Investment Trust.

First let me say I did not set out to write a book. This is how the book came about.

I strongly believe that in any organisation, internal corporate communication is as important as external communication. People in the company would like to know what is happening to the company and what the management and leaders are thinking about. How are we doing? What's happening next? What are our vision, strategy, and value system like?

At CapitaLand, I conduct quarterly staff briefings immediately after the quarterly financial results announcement. How have we done during the last quarter and what are we going to do next quarter or for the rest of the year? I also hold breakfast or lunch sessions with groups of colleagues to get their feedback and to assess their potential.

Another communication channel that I have adopted is to write rather informal "story-telling" emails to the staff. I do this once in a while during three- to four-hour sessions on Sunday afternoons in the complete quiet of my office, waffling and tossing about, with my limited vocabulary and poor grammar, some private thoughts or interesting recent encounters.

These emails usually centre on our corporate events, vision, value systems, ethos, corporate cultures, strategies, challenges to our survival and business ideas.

I believe that CEOs and leaders could do well to make known their thoughts, ideas, concerns and encounters so that the people they lead can be closer to them mentally and emotionally. A common culture can be forged subconsciously in this manner, and story-telling can be an effective and powerful tool for this type of sharing.

I have since 1998 discovered that I enjoy writing these Sunday afternoon emails very much—even at the expense of my Sunday afternoon nine-hole golf games. Given more time, if I were not travelling for work during weekends, I would love to write more.

Over the years, there have been many suggestions from staff that I compile these emails into a book. However, I did not take up the suggestion as I thought it unnecessary to do so, since these emails can be retrieved from our company intranet anytime.

Beginning this year, we made the decision to create and build our own in-house management and leadership development institute. It is called CLIMB—CapitaLand Institute of Management and Business. We acquired an old historical building on Sentosa and spent several million dollars converting it into a modern training facility. The institute offers four main modules—orientation for new hires, general management, leadership development, and finally, but most importantly, our corporate value alignment.

CLIMB is managed by a full-time principal—Lynda Wee—and her staff, with training conducted by both external lecturers and our in-house senior staff, including myself. This book will be used as reading material for CLIMB participants to catch up on past emails. I have pledged all royalties from this book to the CapitaLand Hope Foundation, which is a charity foundation formed by CapitaLand to help provide needy and underprivileged children with homes, education and medical care.

I think investing in CLIMB is the best investment we have made in CapitaLand. It is investing in our future. It is in this spirit that I've decided to compile my emails into a book. This book can help CLIMB communicate CapitaLand's core values and corporate culture to all staff. I hope readers outside of the CapitaLand family will find it useful as well.

Liew Mun Leong
Group President & CEO
CapitaLand Limited
November 2007

Chapter 1

The Three Ps –
The Keys to Success

"If you don't have discipline, you can't do anything great. If you don't have discipline, you can't be a CEO."

M y career has taken me from being a government civil engineer working on the construction of Changi Airport in the '70s to becoming the head of an international real estate company with a S$20 billion (US$12.5 billion) market capitalisation. It hasn't always been plain sailing, and along the way I've encountered professional hardship, sometimes working in very difficult situations. Yet, I've never given up.

I'm often asked what the keys are behind my success. I started to reflect on this at a time when I was reading *Only the Paranoid Succeed* by Andrew Grove, the former chairman of Intel. Like him, I believe in the value of paranoia. Maybe I am born with it. In business you've got to plan and be prepared for every eventuality. This is especially true in a cyclical business like real estate.

In that respect it is a very Singaporean character trait. Paranoia is just another word for what we call "*Kiasu*" (怕输) in a Chinese dialect. Such paranoia was also ingrained in me early on in my career, because civil engineers (like me) focus on nature's challenges and the environment, and as such we must be prepared for nature's unexpected forces, be it the "one-in-a-hundred-years" storm or the earthquake in a seismic zone.

Perseverance is another key to my success. Few people realise that I actually have a problem with heights: I get vertigo. Yet, this has never deterred me from climbing to the top of a tall building to inspect construction work that I had to supervise. Professionally, I've often been told "you can't do this in this business". For example, I was told "you cannot export real estate", but I've persevered and today, CapitaLand is successful in more than 100 cities in over 20 countries. In 2001, CapitaLand tried unsuccessfully to launch the first Singaporean REIT (real estate investment trust), the SingMall Property Trust. We faced a host of challenges from the onset, from constraints within the regulatory framework to overcoming market perception of the product's viability. The first REIT IPO (initial public offering) was undersubscribed and the flotation had to be cancelled. Yet, CapitaLand refused to give up. We launched CapitaMall Trust the following year and this time it worked. That was how we pioneered REITs in Singapore. Today, we are the leader in this REITs market. Perseverance will take you through.

I'm also a perfectionist; again, this comes down to my professional training. Engineers are very meticulous. We measure our work and we measure our errors to improve until we reach perfection. When you do something it needs to fit. There is no room for error. Some people will also say I'm very fussy on details, but ultimately it's a reflection on me and the company if a job is not well done. Call it personal pride.

Of course, everybody has his own roots of success, but this is what has made me who I am today. So Paranoia, Perseverance and Perfectionism, that's my philosophy of success!

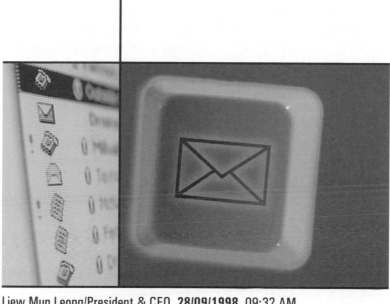

Liew Mun Leong/President & CEO **28/09/1998** 09:32 AM

To: All Staff

cc: Board of Directors

bcc:

Subject: **Persevering to Stay on Top**

Cap/taLand

... Building People

Dear Colleagues,

Two years ago, we set ourselves the audacious goal of transforming Pidemco Land into a world-class property company. At that time, our economy was growing, the property market was skyrocketing and the going was good. We were all euphoric.

Alas, the honeymoon was brief!

In July last year, the Thai baht started falling and economic turmoil quickly engulfed the region. This merciless economic cancer has permeated across the whole of Asia, threatening even stable and developed economies. Even with political stability and sound economic fundamentals, we cannot escape the coming recessionary forces. What about our goal now? Do we stop "beating our chest" and give up our dream? No, we shouldn't. We must persevere and sustain all our ongoing efforts to make Pidemco Land a world-class company. Maybe it will take longer, but we can do it. How do we do it?

Recently, over lunch, an ex-banker very cleverly suggested to me that we now have the golden opportunity to build Pidemco Land into "a strong company in a weak market". That inspired me.

Building "a strong company in a weak market" is a strategic statement. We are, no doubt, in a weak market, but we also have the potential to build a strong company. We shouldn't miss this chance. If we can build a strong company in this weak market, then when the market turns for the better (and it should happen, it's just a question of timing), we will already have it made!

Highly successful developers like Li Ka Shing,[1] Kwek Hong Png[2] and Ng Teng Fong[3] all had that vision and they bravely took it forward despite falling confidence in the property market. They took strategic advantage of the then recessionary property market in the 1960s and built on it. We now call it counter-cyclical investment! Look at their success! Was it a gamble for them? No, it was their vision, entrepreneurship, hard work, perseverance and their own form of management style that brought them through. Of course, times were different then. Nowadays, we need more than vision and bravery; we also need much more sophisticated investment management skills!

We have done a fair bit during the last two years to improve the company. I believe we have built a strong team. But our business environment is dynamic and we must change and improve continuously. We have developed a management "framework" to build a world-class company and I have appointed four teams to work out the plans to achieve this. When preparations are ready, we will brief you on how we all have to work together to reach our goal. Remember, we must have a plan!

But even if we succeed in building up a strong company, how do we stay on top? Can we weather another economic storm? I once read a statement from Johnny Shih, chairman of Asustek Computer Inc. in Taiwan. He said that the only way to stay on top is to be a Perfectionist and be Paranoid at the same time. How true!

But that is not enough. The current adverse economy reminds me that there is one more factor that will be equally critical in our journey to reach the top and stay there: we must also have Perseverance. There should be no let-up, no "weak knees". If we can't persevere, we won't reach the top, let alone stay there!

I therefore suggest that to reach a world-class standard and remain on top, we must be a Perfectionist and be Paranoid, and we must Persevere—the 3Ps.

Kindest,
Liew Mun Leong

End Notes

1 Li Ka Shing is one of Hong Kong's most famous businessmen. Presently, he is the chairman of Hutchison Whampoa Limited (HWL) and Cheung Kong Holdings in Hong Kong.

2 Kwek Hong Png was the late founder of Hong Leong Group in Singapore, which now has in its stable of companies City Development Limited, an international property and hotel conglomerate.

3 Ng Teng Fong is Singapore's real estate billionaire. Today, he is one of Hong Kong's largest real estate developers, and his Far East Organisation is one of the largest landholders in Singapore.

Liew Mun Leong/President & CEO **12/10/1998** 10:09 AM

   To: All Staff

   cc: Board of Directors

  bcc:

Subject: **Perfection is a Mental Discipline**

CapitaLand

... Building People

I once asked Ang Swee Kee[1] what standard of cleanliness we can expect from our cleaning contractors when they clean our commercial buildings and car parks everyday. We specify the frequency of cleaning, but the acceptable standard of cleanliness seems relative.

One morning in Geneva, I observed a man cleaning the pavement next to the hotel where I was staying. His standard was not only to sweep away the litter from the pavement. Whenever he saw sticky patches (e.g. chewing gum), he would take out a little spade from his side pocket and carefully remove these ugly contaminations before he brushed them off. This is the standard I think we should adopt. Most of our cleaners just ignore such "sticky problems". Ang Swee Kee told me that cleaners nowadays don't carry a little spade in their trousers anymore. "Why not," I asked, "if he really wishes to do his job well". A small effort, but it is a matter of mental discipline.

Last week, I met another perfectionist. Chris Wallis is a specialist building consultant for Four Seasons Hotels & Resorts. He has spent 28 years with Four Seasons, having built almost 40 hotels all over the world. Today, Four Seasons hotels are rated top of the rank among five-star hotels. That's why we chose them as our management operator for our hotel in Canary Wharf, London. After meeting Chris Wallis one afternoon (and "crossing swords" with him gently), I now know why Four Seasons is world class. He is a classic example of a perfectionist. Very, very experienced, he knows absolutely all the standards for a good five-star hotel—from the size of a bathtub and how long it should take to fill it, the plumbing, the thickness of the wallpaper, the curtains, the furniture and fixtures in the rooms and restaurants, back-room equipment, right down even to the design of the electric switches. Our famous interior designer perfected a beautiful light switch for him to approve. He looked and played with it in his hand swiftly and said it was good, but pointed out that the noise level during off/on switching must be reduced. Nothing about a five-star hotel seemed to escape him. We are happy to have a specialist like him, but our problem is that we need to control costs and have only 66 weeks to build this five-star hotel (in time for the new millennium). Vice presidents Patricia Chia[2] and Poon Hin Kong have been given strict orders from me to keep to budget and time. They are now struggling (actually fighting?) with him to balance his adamantly perfectionist call for high standards. So what price are we willing to pay and how long can we delay our five-star hotel to get it perfect? As the hotel operator, he wants his unwavering high standards to be met. As the investor, however, we must make our judgement call.

What about making mistakes and learning from them? I have another recent interesting anecdote. We formed a joint-property fund company with ING (Dutch banking and I was talking with our partner, the chairman of ING Real Estate, Jan Doets about the qualifications required for the recruitment of the managing director. I proposed that the candidate should meet five requirements:

(i)   the right academic qualifications
      (business degree, CFA, etc)
(ii) good experience in real estate
(iii) a track record in fund management
(iv) a high degree of integrity
(v)   a team player

I thought I was thorough and tough on my requirements. Doets told me that he had one more requirement. The candidate must have made a mistake and failed before. To him, having failed before is an important qualification that would make him feel confident he could manage our fund. If he has not failed before, he has not learnt enough and his first big mistake may be with us. I agree with him.

End Notes

1 Ang Swee Kee was then Managing Director of PREMAS International, Pidemco Land's property services arm.
2 Patricia Chia is now CEO of CapitaLand Residential Singapore.

Liew Mun Leong/President & CEO **17/10/1998** 12:52 PM

To:	**All Staff**
cc:	**Board of Directors**
bcc:	
Subject:	**Being a Perfectionist**

Cap/taLand

... Building People

T his week, let me relate two personal nostalgic stories about being a perfectionist.

In 1978, during my airport construction days, I was supervising a Japanese contruction company (Obayashi Gumi) for the laying of the first concrete pavement for aircraft parking at Changi Airport. The Japanese site engineer was a man called Mr T Sakai.

At that time, we had just introduced an automatic paving machine to lay high-quality pavement concrete (360mm thick and very expensive concrete because of the high cement content). Both Sakai and I were relatively new to that paving technology and we got the American supplier to operate the monstrous and complicated automatic paving machine.

After several trials and errors, we started the first day of paving and completed 100 metres of concreting. High speed! At the end of the day, I did the final detailed inspection. I found the paving to be satisfactory, but there were some minor irregularities on the surface.

The concrete was still "wet" and I suggested that Sakai get several skilled masons to improve these irregularities by hand. He surprisingly rejected my idea and instead insisted that the whole 100-metre length of pavement concrete be removed and re-paved. I was really taken aback as I felt that it was a waste of one day's work and the destroyed concrete would cost the Japanese company S$40,000 (US$17,620) (if I remember correctly). And he would have a lot of explaining to do to his supervisors in Tokyo! However, he stood firm and pointedly told me that his concrete pavement must look good and last for a long, long time. With a very serious expression, he said he did not want his grandchildren to land in Changi Airport one day and for someone to criticise that their grandfather did such poor work. So, he sent a bulldozer to remove the whole strip of concrete. It was a painful sight to see expensive, good quality concrete rejected just because of some irregular surface finishes. The next paving, and thereafter, the job was very well done. This year, 20 years later, I caught up with him in Osaka. I asked him if he would have repeated the same stubborn attitude today. He said "Yes" and he was very proud of himself, insisting on his standard of quality. He is a perfectionist—it is pride again.

My second anecdote is more personal, as it relates to the modest experience of my late father. He migrated from China as a young lad, with little education and absolutely no training. For his entire life here, he worked as a fitter, operating on a lathe machine (machining steel components for a ship repair company). He was charming to us, but he was an obese person—and physically clumsy in many ways. Yet, he was a master-fitter and could machine metal components to a few microns' tolerance (the thickness of a strand of hair). His boss liked his work and gave him much-welcomed overtime tasks that brought in bonus earnings. When I was studying in a technical secondary school, I had to learn how to use a lathe machine. It was very difficult even as a nimble teenage boy and I wondered how my father could produce such precision work. With his large and rather clumsy hands, how could he still produce such precision engineering pieces, I once asked him. "It was years of hard training and a matter of discipline", he explained. He philosophically reflected that he had no choice but to develop the mental discipline to do it. He did it for a living so that we could survive. He lamented: "In the family, there is only one person working but seven mouths eating. If I stop my hands, all of you have to stop your mouths". It is about mind over body if we are to train to perfect our skills to survive. I shall never forget that piece of advice for survival.

That was a crude, early, simple message to me about training and mental discipline to learn difficult skills against our natural inclination or disposition, in order to survive.

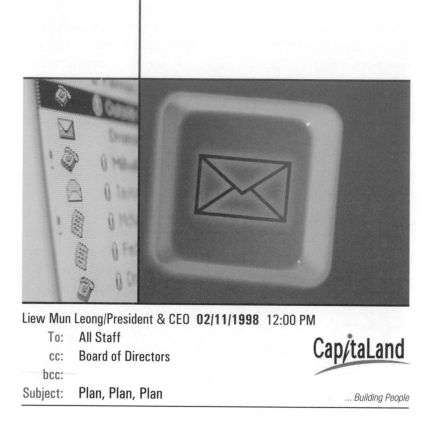

Liew Mun Leong/President & CEO **02/11/1998** 12:00 PM

  To: All Staff

  cc: Board of Directors

  bcc:

Subject: **Plan, Plan, Plan**

Cap/taLand

... Building People

I agree with Johnny Shih, chairman of Asustek Computer Inc., that to stay on top, we need to be paranoid. Why? The answer is simple. It is the Singaporean's natural way of thinking, one that I agree with.

"Paranoia" is simply a sophisticated English word for the Singaporean habit called "kiasu". Many successes for us in Singapore have been due to this "kiasu" mindset, from the days when we went to school, then university, or did our national (military) service. It is ingrained in our lifestyle and often becomes apparent when we play games, go for holidays and even when we "attack" the buffet table (as it is only one price!).

It is when you are paranoid that you plan—and plan for the worst situations. For example, it is in envisaging the worst-case scenario that Asians prepare for "rainy days". They develop a high rate of savings. It is this paranoia that makes us prepare ourselves for the worst in life. It is this paranoia that spurs us to "pre-experience" and prepare for what can turn out unexpectedly. In management, we call this "Murphy's Law", which pessimistically says that if something can fail, it will (and usually at the wrong time).

Don't underestimate Murphy's Law. Let me give you a recent personal experience. As a former president of ISO (the International Organisation of Standardisation), I was invited to give a dinner talk on ISO to an audience of 500. It was a big and grand event and I spent tremendous effort, working with Sok Kheng[1] (over several weekends!) to prepare some 80 slides. I was eventually satisfied with my preparations—there were beautiful pictures and slides on the history of ISO, etc. But what happened on the very morning of the talk? I completely lost my voice! It was a very painful and frustrating experience, not for the sound I could barely make, but for the little I could do with my slides! Wasted! I rushed to the doctor and pumped in antibiotics hoping that by evening, my voice would recover! It did a little and I braced myself on stage and forced it out! I learnt my lesson—don't endanger your voice (or your health) near D-Day!

Another example is how I always arrive at the airport at least one and a half to two hours before departure time. In 20 years of business travelling, I have not missed a single flight and therefore have not missed a single meeting overseas. I have never missed any early morning meeting when overseas because I habitually set two alarm clocks (my own and the one in my hotel room, which I don't really trust) plus the hotel's wake-up call service. The army calls it the second degree of redundancy. I have never lost my air ticket, wallet (which my daughter has, after just one year of business travel) or passport as I safely button them up in my coat (touch wood!). I am quite absent-minded, but I am extremely prudent on such personal matters—paranoid if you like to call it!

I often tell foreigners that one reason for Singapore's success is our propensity to plan. We plan, plan and plan. Is it paranoia?

From my days in the civil service, I know how much we plan and to what detail we plan. I will tell you of one situation we planned for, which I thought was paranoid at that time. In 1987, when I was in PWD,[2] I was assigned to participate in a National Planning Committee chaired by the permanent secretary of the Ministry of Home Affairs. It was a co-ordination meeting to plan for a disaster scenario. The scenario: a jumbo 747 aircraft carrying 500 passengers had crashed into a few HDB[3] blocks. It sounded terribly remote and paranoid! What would our action plan be? Plenty of operational details were worked out, from how to get the passenger list and reach the passengers' families, to the technical details of how to salvage casualties from the rubble of the building, the type of rescue equipment, the number of ambulances, hospitals' responses, etc.

At that time, I thought, "God, we are mad to imagine that. We are paranoid." But I painstakingly sat through the planning exercise. Guess what happened? One year later, when I was in Rotterdam, Holland, an aircraft did exactly what we envisaged could happen. The plane had actually crashed into a tall building in the city! It was world news. I told my Dutch friends that although this seemed like a very remote event, we in Singapore had actually thought about such an accident and had developed a response and rescue plan. I'm not sure if they believed me.

Postscript: That's also what happened on 9/11!

End Notes

1 Chia Sok Kheng is Liew Mun Leong's executive personal assistant.
2 PWD stands for Public Works Department, a former Singapore government statutory board, which has now been privatised and renamed CPG Corporation.
3 HDB is the Housing Development Board, the statutory board of the Singapore Ministry of National Development, responsible for public housing in Singapore.

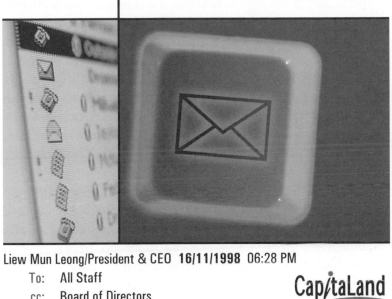

Liew Mun Leong/President & CEO **16/11/1998** 06:28 PM

To:	All Staff
cc:	Board of Directors
bcc:	
Subject:	**Remember Murphy's Law!**

Cap/taLand

... Building People

R emember Murphy's law—"If something can go wrong, it will go wrong". When it comes down to investing billions of dollars in a project, one should be aggressive and decisive, but also paranoid. The world is not what it seems to be.

Many of you may be surprised that I talk so much about being paranoid. But I am only suggesting that we should be fully aware of the negative impact of unexpected events. It is a preparation of the mind—to be guarded whilst we can be decisive and move along quickly. Speed is important in business and we must be prepared for the worst to happen so that we can make a U turn and survive.

Being prudent, or paranoid, is also valid for our investments.

So far, since we took over Pidemco Land,[1] we have not been further exposed to the economic turmoil in other Asian countries. Even during the heyday, when property prices were going up in Asia, we held our hands firmly. We didn't put anything in Thailand, the Philippines, Indonesia (we intended to put 5% of a project in Jakarta but pulled out just in time!), China (though we had existing projects before) or Hong Kong, although we have been exploring all these markets seriously. We invested in one freehold condominium project in Kuala Lumpur, but we have already sold more than 40% of it. Instead, we shifted our investments to safer (I hope) and more mature locations like London.

I will tell you an anecdote. Kui Seng[2] and I were going to Hong Kong frequently to study the market there. We decided after a good nine months' research to participate in a land auction. We worked with our Hong Kong partners ("steady" people) and did plenty of ground research including visiting the tender site and its vicinity during day time and at night time to watch the activities around it. I never want to buy any land/property unless I have personally seen it, walked around and talked to the people living around it. Due diligence must be more than paper analysis. Together with our Hong Kong partners we worked out our bid price of HK$4.2 billion for the land (about S$850 million). We went to the auction that morning ready to stretch to HK$4.5 billion, if need be, because we were all passionate about securing that beautiful piece of land. Alas! We could not even reach the semi-final. The final successful price was a hefty HK$6.02 billion. Just about HK$2 billion, or S$400 million, more than our boldest move. No heroes' welcome for us!

What happened? Were we too prudent? The "winner" is now going to lose big money with the land costing so much. Nobody could have predicted the world crisis coming so fast and so deep. Of course, who knows—land prices may jump back and then the winner will be the wiser one.

Another story. Last year (before the crisis) in May we were tendering to buy land for some executive condominium[3] (EC) projects. We worked out our sums and the price was decided and approved. The day before the tender closed, which was a holiday here (Vesak Day), I was still pondering over our agreed price for one site. I came back quietly into the office to go through the figures again, not knowing Teck Koon[4] had the same paranoia—we wanted to win five EC sites, but we were afraid of paying too much. He too had come back and was in his office to rework the sums. Each of us didn't know the other person was in the office. The next morning we met at the 11th hour, shared our paranoia and cut some S$8 million (US$4.7 million) from our original agreed price. Guess what, we lost one tender but won another one—the one we cut S$8 million on! It may mean that either our sums were not well done or we had not read our competition accurately. Lord Buddha[5] was kind as we saved S$8 million, but in hindsight, he could have been kinder by making us lose the tender as we still lost money on the EC project!

End Notes

1 Liew Mun Leong was appointed as president and CEO of Pidemco Land in 1996. In 2000, Pidemco Land's parent company Singapore Technologies acquired a controlling stake in DBS Land, the property arm of DBS group. The two companies, which often competed against each other, were merged to create a new single entity: CapitaLand. It was listed in November 2000.
2 Tham Kui Seng was then senior vice president (overseas investment), Pidemco Land. He is now chief corporate officer of CapitaLand.
3 Executive Condominiums (ECs) were introduced by the Singapore government to cater to Singaporeans, especially young graduates and professionals who can afford more than an HDB flat but find private property out of their reach. ECs are comparable in design and facilities to private condominiums as they are developed and sold by private developers.
4 Kee Teck Koon was then senior vice president (Singapore investment), Pidemco Land. He is now the chief investment officer of CapitaLand and deputy chairman of CapitaLand Commercial and Integrated Development Limited, CapitaLand Retail Limited and CapitaLand Financial Limited.
5 Liew Mun Leong refers to Lord Buddha as the email was written and the recalculation was done during the Buddhist Vesak Day celebrations.

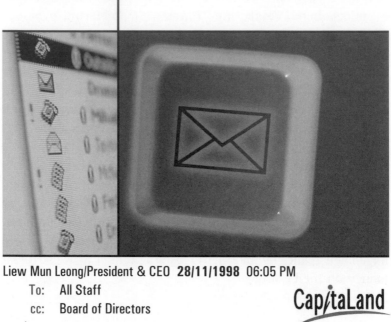

Liew Mun Leong/President & CEO **28/11/1998** 06:05 PM

To:	All Staff
cc:	Board of Directors
bcc:	
Subject:	**Paranoia in Business**

Cap/taLand

... Building People

T here is a strong linkage between my paranoia and my background training as a civil engineer. Civil engineering is a very old engineering discipline—probably the oldest. It started in the Stone Age era when man first put a tree trunk across a river to cross it—civil engineers now call it bridge engineering.

As much of civil engineering focuses on challenging nature and the environment, a civil engineer has to be paranoid of nature and its unexpected forces.

When a civil engineer designs a tall building, for example, he has to incorporate a large "factor of safety" in both the design and construction phases. There are large safety margins to consider in loading, unexpected usage, strength of building materials, the foundations, the construction method and natural forces, like wind load, earthquakes, etc. At the end of the day, the civil engineer has to be paranoid about all the possible negative factors and yet, God forbid, it still may fail!

Another classic example is when we build a storm-water drain: it has to be large enough to take the worst possible storm of "once in a hundred years"! This means that the engineer will dig out data from long-term statistics and design the drain to cater for that eventuality. When I first brought some American civil engineers to Changi Airport's construction site many years ago, they were amazed and laughingly asked me why I was constructing large canals in the airport. They were airport drains that have to cater for Singapore's heavy rainfall intensity and the Americans never appreciated how much rain falls on us here in the tropics.

When we were building the Changi runway and aircraft parking apron, a large part of the soil there (about 70%) was underlain with marine clay. Marine clay is notoriously soft and compressible, and if something is built on it, the structure will settle gradually over time. We predicted that in time, our runway would sink in some places more than 1½ metres down! We were "paranoid" of a sinking runway and spent millions of dollars treating this underlying soil before we built our runway system on top of it. Interestingly, when the Malaysians were building or rebuilding the Penang runway at that time, they ignored this possible long-term settlement problem. We were questioned by the Civil Aviation Authority of Singapore why we "pumped" so much money below the ground to stabilise the soil. We wanted to avoid a sinking runway, and with all our civil engineering skills, invested millions of dollars underground to prevent future settlement.

During that time, treatment of soil was my responsibility and engineering specialty. I learnt and enjoyed soil mechanics so much that I named my son (who was just born then) Karl after the "Father of Soil Mechanics", Karl Terzake (a German civil engineer). I had big hopes, but Karl did not turn out to be a civil engineer!

Subsequently, the Penang runway indeed settled and their engineers came to learn our paranoid tricks. I am glad that even after more than 17 years of operation our runway is not a roller coaster!

Similarly, when we build a large building, we have to provide for many contingencies, no matter how remote they may be. Many standby arrangements are made to ensure that we have no breakdown in services. No matter how well we are trained, we may not be able to anticipate the forces that cause a burst dam, a failed bridge or a change in weather like El Nino, which is currently causing extensive floods in many countries.

Many catastrophes and accidents are caused by unexpected events converging simultaneously. It is a convergence of a number of unexpected events that caused the failure of Hotel New World,[1] the Sentosa cable car[2] and the collapse of Jalan Eunos Bridge during construction. When we completed the taxiway bridge at Changi Airport some 15 years ago and we first witnessed a large jumbo jet crossing the ECP,[3] I was quietly quite nervous. We had had all the design checked and the construction was tightly supervised. but had we been paranoid enough?

The moral of the story is that in our management of business, we must learn to visualise what can possibly turn against us so that we have some "pre-experience" of the situation and can develop some fall-back or contingency plans.

The Chinese have a saying: "not to be afraid of ten thousand events but to watch out for the one-in-a-ten-thousand event" (不怕一万，只怕万一). The Chinese are indeed good civil engineers—they built the Great Wall (paranoid about invasions by the barbarians!) some 2,000 years ago and it is still standing!

End Notes

1 The Hotel New World in Singapore, a one-star budget hotel, collapsed on 15 March 1986, killing 33 people.
2 On 29 January 1983, tragedy struck when the towering structure of a Panamanian-registered oil rig struck the cable of the Sentosa Cable Car and caused two cable cars to plunge into the sea. The oil rig became entangled in the cable and caused it to snap. It also left thirteen people trapped in four other cable cars between Mount Faber and Sentosa. A total of seven people died in the cable car tragedy.
3 ECP is East Coast Parkway, an expressway that leads to Changi Airport.

Liew Mun Leong/President & CEO **12/12/1998** 05:18 PM

   To: All Staff

   cc: Board of Directors

   bcc:

Subject: **Perseverance is the Genius in Disguise**

Cap/taLand

... Building People

L et me tell you an inspiring story about perseverance and success.

During the mid-80s, Barry S. Sternlicht, a young, twenty-something Harvard MBA graduate struggled through a few rather difficult years in London's property business. It was a prolonged down market and nothing moved. Finally, he left London to seek employment in the US. A then potential employer, whom I met recently, interviewed him but selected an alternative candidate instead, probably because of his lack of a network in the US. Today, just 10 years later, Barry Sternlicht is fabulously called (even by the potential employer who didn't employ him) the "King of the Universe". At the young age of 37, Barry successfully acquired two large hotel groups—all within two months—in July and August last year. He is now president of the Starwood Group, which owns the entire empire of the Westin and Sheraton groups, making his company the largest hotel operator group in the world. He is reputed to have swung both deals within a two-month interval, fighting against such giant competitors as the Hilton Group—an intense modern commercial drama of David against Goliath. The reward was more than 200 five-star Westin and Sheraton hotels all over the world. Barry persevered and succeeded to the surprise of many.

I met Barry briefly in Washington this year. He struck me as a quiet but determined man. He looked hawkish and knew exactly what he wanted. He was interviewed recently on our local TV programme *In Conversation*. When asked the secret of his success in his US$16 billion acquisition of the Sheraton group, his one-word answer was "Perseverance". In any negotiation, he said, the key word is "Perseverance". He summed up: "Perseverance is the genius in disguise." I believe him.

Think about it. Isn't perseverance an important key success factor for many things in life—be it learning a hobby, running a marathon, studying for an examination, undergoing training for a special skill, climbing up a career ladder, developing a business, or for that matter, scouting for and chasing after a life-long companion? Perseverance calls for a host of personal traits including will power and determination, patience and tolerance, and a high threshold for pain. It needs tenacity and courage too. Nothing great can be achieved without perseverance.

The property business follows economic cycles of ups and downs. If we cannot persevere, we will never be able to ride through the down-market cycle. In which case, you will never live to see the up market again. Property business needs perseverance and "weak knees" will never do. Perseverance is required in any business. All businesses need to be developed and built and then patiently managed for the light to appear at the end of the often very long and dark tunnel.

I am sure each of us has our own personal stories to tell, how we persevered before we reached a milestone of success. As a company, we need to have a high degree of perseverance during bad times (or even good times) before we can reach a truly world-class company status. We will have to work hard, work smart and work fast, but we cannot despair and let up when we need to ride through the difficult times to prepare for market recovery. Even from then on, we need to persevere again to remain on top.

Moral of the story: Never say die!

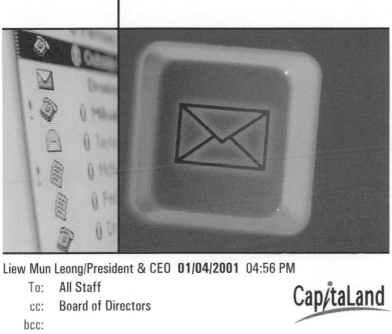

Liew Mun Leong/President & CEO **01/04/2001** 04:56 PM

To: All Staff

cc: Board of Directors

bcc:

Subject: **Corporate Discipline Starts with the Smallest Details**

Cap/taLand

... Building People

R ecently some of you may have felt that I have been very tough and demanding on the little details. Yes, I have been difficult and fastidious—censuring poor telephone manners, demanding faster submission of minutes of meetings, standardising formats of board papers including their font size, chasing for faster circulation of resolutions and earlier board papers, checking on overseas travelling and insisting on which class of hotels to use. I even criticised littering in our toilets (for goodness sake, some of us don't even know how to use the nice tissue paper provided in the dispensers!) and how inefficiently our seminar refreshments had been organised.

So why all this fuss from the CEO? Corporate discipline!

Corporate discipline and high standards should be observed from small details onwards. I'll tell you a couple of small but ridiculous stories. Last month when I was in London, I saw my daughter off one evening from Euston railway station to Manchester. The train was scheduled to leave at 8pm. At just about 8pm, when I was saying goodbye to her, an announcement came. "We are now ready to depart for Manchester but our driver has not arrived. The train will depart as soon as he arrives". Our all-important driver came at 8:26pm. I was cursing, but my daughter calmly suggested to me that delays like these were not uncommon. How ridiculous!

The train had 10 coaches with a few hundred anxious, paying passengers. They had to wait for an ill-disciplined, late driver—a complete breakdown of corporate discipline. In Singapore, the driver, his supervisor and manager would all have been fired. I related this to Sir Alan Cockshaw[1] (our board member). He told me he once boarded a train that was delayed a few hours—because there was no engine in the train. It was sent out for repairs and it did not get back to the train.

Airlines in Europe and the US are no better. My recent trip from London to Amsterdam with a flying time of less than an hour got delayed for more than two hours both ways. The airline staff happily opened the gate after our long wait—no explanation, no forewarning of the delay, no new flight time given, no apology, nothing abnormal had happened to them— except paying passengers suffering in silence. We were late for our scheduled meetings in both Amsterdam and London, a first for me!

American flights—no joy! We were flying from Chicago to Los Angeles. Without notice, the flight was cancelled and we were only told by our friend who had checked the flight time for us. We telephoned to change our flight for a later one. When we arrived at the airport, the flight had not been cancelled after all, but by then we had lost our seats. We complained and got them back, but later that flight and the subsequent one were cancelled. No announcement—you had to watch the monitor yourself. We learnt our lesson and watched the monitor every minute. We jumped onto the next available flight after a big fight with the airline. The airline staff rudely told us: "I am trying to help you!" Help us? Who was creating the problem and who was the paying customer? Another check-in counter staff told Richard Helfer,[2] who was travelling with me: "If you complain so much, go change and use another airline!" We couldn't—there wasn't any flying to LA that time of the night. We left our hotel in Chicago at 3:30pm and got into Los Angeles at 1:30am (Chicago time).

The excuse given was bad weather—but we were flying on the same day from New York to Chicago and then Los Angeles and there wasn't any bad weather anywhere to be seen! Later on, I read that the public is demanding airlines be more accountable for delays. Two bills are now proposed in Congress to make airlines more transparent and accountable for inconveniencing the travelling public and not simply using bad weather as an excuse.

All these unacceptable "slacks" stem from a complete breakdown in corporate discipline.

Mistakes made without lessons learnt and careless employees getting away scot-free. They relax, become recalcitrant, lackadaisical and even more careless. It is a country-club mentality. CapitaLand must never allow such ill discipline and careless thinking to set in. My disciplinarian mother used to tell me that when a tree is young, like a branch, we can twist and bend it. Not when it is a fully grown tree. My job is to set high standards of performance and behaviour—small or big things alike. The corporate culture, for perfection, must be right, from the very start.

End Notes

1 Sir Alan Cockshaw is a former director of CapitaLand.
2 Richard Helfer was then the president and CEO of Raffles Holdings Limited. He left the organisation in early 2003. In 2005, CapitaLand divested its hotels operations.

Liew Mun Leong/President & CEO **12/09/2001** 05:37 PM

To: All Staff

cc: Board of Directors

bcc:

Subject: **Preparing for the Worst—Be Paranoid**

Cap/taLand

... Building People

I n a recent CNBC interview for *Managing Asia*, I was asked a pointed question: "Mr Liew, you worked in the public service for more than 20 years. Some critics commented that you were an administrator and a bureaucrat. What's your response?"

I replied that I believe I had benefited enormously from my 20 years in public service. It taught me how big organisations operate. Things are done systematically. Big organisations require systems planning and systems engineering. They plan out every small operational detail, every minute detail for different scenarios. In a positive way, the public sector in Singapore is very paranoid. Let me give you an example.

In 1985, I was appointed to a national planning committee to work out a national contingency disaster plan, which I then thought was paranoid and would never happen. The scenario was: "A jumbo jet carrying 500 people had crashed into a block of HDB flats."

We had to develop the details of a contingency response plan to meet the crisis. We worked on every minute detail of the rescue operation—number of ambulances, doctors, hospital beds, fire-fighters, engineering plan, plants, tools and other logistics to extricate casualties, blood donations, ways to reach families, etc. I thought we had gone crazy.

Exactly nine months later, I happened to be in Amsterdam and that nightmarish scenario happened—a KLM jumbo jet crashed into a building. I told my Dutch friends then that we had actually just worked on a contingency plan to face such a crisis. They were astounded.

I often extol the virtues of the 3 Ps: Perfectionism, Paranoia and Perseverance. It may be easy to understand the drive to be a perfectionist or to persevere, while many may scoff at the suggestion to be paranoid. But I'd like to point to the book *Only the Paranoid Survive* by the former chairman of Intel, Andrew S. Grove, to support that last point.

Last night, I watched in horror on TV the extraordinary and unbelievably destructive events unfolding at the New York World Trade Centre and at the Pentagon. The difference with our 1985 scenario? It was a much larger scale of destruction and it was meticulously and professionally planned.

Were we paranoid to have envisaged such a disaster some 16 years ago?

My message is—be paranoid! The most untoward event can spring at us, so be prepared. Peace or good times are not appreciated until such traumatic events hit us and fear takes over. Disaster may come as an accident, but it can also be planned by fellow human beings for reasons we will never understand. In business it is the same. We will never fully appreciate what our competitors can do to us and why!

Liew Mun Leong/President & CEO **23/03/2002** 06:02 PM

To: All Staff
cc: Board of Directors
bcc:

Subject: **10 Years' Failure, Lifetime Success**

Cap/taLand

... Building People

I n a recent breakfast chat with some of our younger colleagues I was asked about entrepreneurship and our attitude towards failure. I told them this story:

In 1982, I was entrusted by Philip Yeo (then the permanent secretary in Mindef[1]) to head a top-secret airport project. They sent me 25 fresh engineers, all scholars who graduated from abroad. Patricia Chia and Wen Khai Meng[2] were amongst them. I also had to look for some experienced building professionals to help me out—25 rookie engineers, no matter how clever they were, would not make it.

PWD sent me one with 10 years' experience, but he wasn't highly motivated because he had never been promoted. Being Chinese-educated, I suspected he was not articulate enough to impress his seniors—every letter he wrote had to be vetted by the head of department. And he had never had the opportunity to tackle big or challenging projects. I hesitated to take him. Should I immerse him among the mass of bright-eyed scholar-engineers? Would it discourage him further? I decided to take him in.

I told him that I did not care what he had done for the last 10 years, but he had to show me how he could do faster and bigger things with his past experience. I needed to build a laboratory and fill it with equipment to test my building materials and I needed it in three months' time. Could he build and equip it in three months? He tried, he did it, and won my confidence. I gave him more and more assignments, including guiding the "younger Turks". After one year I wrote a strong report, which got him promoted. He was elated as this was his first promotion ever.

Soon after his promotion he came to see me about a job offered to him by a group of foreign contractors who wanted to tender for the MRT[3] job that had just started then. He was hesitant—he probably did not have enough confidence to take up the job offer. He was also feeling bad about leaving me so soon after I got him back on his feet.

He was given a very good offer as the general manager—much better than his miserable government salary—and the challenge of the private sector. I felt that he could do well in the private sector and it would be a sin to just keep him inside. I bravely told him that if he failed, I would take him back. I encouraged him to go.

He went and has since been doing very well in the construction and other investment businesses, and later became part owner of the firm. Now he is doing social and community work, winning all the PBMs,[4] and is a Justice of the Peace. I am sure he is a much wealthier man than me—I know he stays in a much larger house and he never declines if I ask him to donate something to charity!

This man has won his own success and persevered, notwithstanding his weakness and initial 10 years of failure. Never accept failure. Encouraging? Try again!

End Notes

1 Mindef stands for Ministry of Defence in Singapore.
2 Wen Khai Meng is now co-CEO of CapitaLand Financial Limited.
3 MRT stands for Mass Rapid Transit.
4 PBM stands for Pingat Bakti Masyarakat, a public service award conferred by the Singapore government.

Chapter 2

From MICE to ICE – Fighting Competition

"If you can't stand the competition, get out of the business."

"We have got strengths and we have got weaknesses, but so have our competitors, and if we pit our strengths against their weaknesses, we will win."

H eroic Chinese generals used to think they could "Fight 100 battles and win 100 victories" (百战百胜). I used to think like that, too, but in a fiercely competitive global market,

longer the case. You will win some and lose some. The
to make sure you can be mainly on the winning side
and only lose a few.

In 2006, CapitaLand was fiercely competing against
giant gaming operators like Las Vegas Sands and Harrah's
Entertainment. We were bidding for the licence to operate the
first integrated resort in Singapore with a casino component.

We lost the bid for the Marina Bay site in May of that year,
partly because our proposal was not enterprising enough. But
maybe as a silver lining, this loss also helped us crystallise
ideas on how to fight competition, ideas that I had mulled over
since 2002.

A management retreat in Chengdu, China, over the
summer saw some intensive brain storming on the topic of
staying fit in a competitive world. By the end of the two days,
it had become clear to us that to beat international competition,
we had to be Innovative, Creative and Entrepreneurial. That's
how our ICE concept came about.

I am totally convinced that whilst a company may have
built up extensive management skill sets, promoting an ICE
frame of mind will be a strong differentiating factor to help
our company to stay ahead and compete.

In his latest book *Mindset*, John Naisbitt argues that
"You don't get results by solving problems, but by exploiting
opportunities." This is an idea I fully embrace.

Being more innovative, more creative, is important, but
being entrepreneurial is also key. "Management by precedence"
is a convenient and lazy way of doing things for defensive
executives and is for those who are afraid to fail. Coming
up with bold, innovative ideas and having the guts to follow
them through will place the company in good shape to have
more wins than losses.

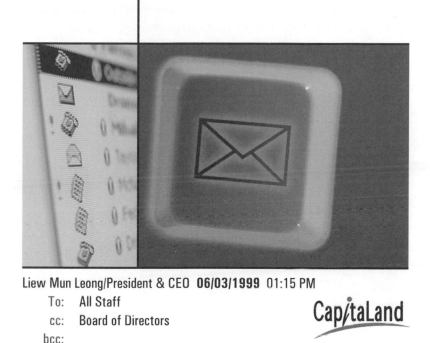

Liew Mun Leong/President & CEO **06/03/1999** 01:15 PM
> To: All Staff
> cc: Board of Directors
> bcc:

Subject: **Five Frogs on a Log**

Cap/taLand

... Building People

A few days ago, I bought an interesting book from a bookstore in San Francisco. It is a serious management book on mergers, acquisitions and the importance of managing the transition period. The title is mischievously called *Five Frogs on a Log* by two writers from PricewaterhouseCoopers.

Besides my affection for frogs, I was intrigued by the title of the book. What are the five frogs doing on the log? It's an inspiration from a riddle that goes like this: Five frogs were sitting on a log. Four decided to jump. Can you guess how many remain on the log? Answer: Five frogs.

Why? Because there is a difference between decision and action! I read a few chapters on the plane on my way back.

They talked about their research on why many companies that acquired or merged with other companies failed. It is about fast actions during that transition period. Companies can postulate big plans to increase shareholder value in terms of synergy, acquiring skills sets, bigger market share, big name, etc. The authors explained that failure is likely if the transition period is not managed well and quickly. The company can decide, but if fast actions are not taken during the transition period, the mergers or acquisitions will not fulfill the euphoric plan set out in the acquisition. Good staff walk away, the market share never grows and the extra profit never comes in. Only lawyers and investment bankers win! And your competitors who take your staff away.

The message is that we can do all our planning, strategic analysis or intellectualising, yet the expected results will not be achieved if we plan, decide but don't ACT fast. The emphasis is on action and speed. We can learn a lot from frogs! They have survived on this planet for 200 million years!

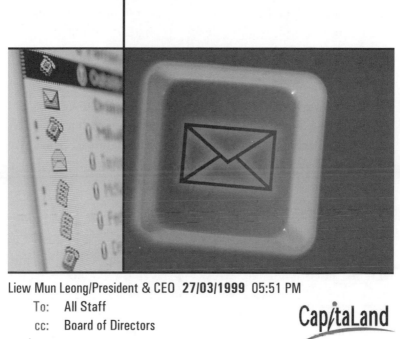

Liew Mun Leong/President & CEO **27/03/1999** 05:51 PM

To: All Staff

cc: Board of Directors

bcc:

Subject: **Taking Smart Initiatives**

Cap/taLand

... Building People

I will tell you a little tale about entrepreneurship, speed, productivity and perseverance.

Juice bars (selling juices from fruits, non-fat yogurts, sorbets and ice) are now a hot fad in America. Just like the Starbucks chain, juice bars have hit the US market like a craze. I'd heard about them but wasn't quite sure what they were all about, although I imagined them like our local fruit juice stalls in the hawker centres. One evening last week several colleagues and I visited one of them in Los Angeles to find out what all the fuss was about.

Only manned by three young boys, this juice bar was full of innovative ideas for mixes of all sorts of fruits imaginable, even wheatgrass, which they called "liquid sunlight". Nothing really new in essence, but the concept is well-marketed and promoted. Healthy food and healthy lifestyle! The bar was simple, but designed with bright yuppie colours and music. It is all about design, design, design in fruit combinations and colours. It is also about marketing, marketing and marketing. They even advertised a pre-IPO recruitment exercise for young people to join them. I was impressed. They know what the customers want!

This week, after the usual long and tiring 13-hour overnight flight from Singapore to London, I casually mentioned to Anthony Seah[1] about the fad in the US while we were driven from Heathrow Airport to our hotel. Why can't we bring this juice bar idea to our commercial space in Canary Wharf or even Singapore? Someone can bring the franchise in or model after it. I asked our driver Ray (a forty-something Englishman from our joint-venture Canary Wharf company) whether juice bars had already arrived in London. "Never heard of it, sir", he said, but he would find out. I know Ray to be a very resourceful person and left the subject there.

To my surprise, by the afternoon when Ray picked me up after lunch for the next meeting, he had completed his "business exploration". He reported to me enthusiastically that there was one called "Squeeze" and he knew where it was operating. He said it was owned by an Australian woman and that she would be in at 3pm that day and he could bring us there. He also found out that it was not a franchise. He had gone to recce the place and had secured menu leaflets. The menu was more or less the same as those in the US. He had essentially completed the "business development study"! Unfortunately, we had an extremely busy schedule and couldn't spare the time to share his findings. He appeared disappointed. I thanked and assured him I would see it the next time.

Imagine this English driver's initiative and the speed of action. He knew nothing about the subject but went to the Internet to find out what this was all about. He visited the place straight away when he was waiting for his next driving mission, got the menu and spoke to the people there

—he even found out when the Australian boss was going to be around. All within half a day, he successfully gathered business intelligence about the operation. Can our business development executives work so fast and have the initiative to attain our objective? Granted, Ray used to manage (I was told) a butcher's shop before his business failed and he became a driver. But he has never lost his business acumen and passion for fast business action. Do we have something or somewhere local in London we don't know? Leave it to him and he will find out pretty soon. Want to find somewhere to eat something different, some local historical stuff, or hunt down an unknown music CD? Leave it to him—he delivers the goods. He knows London, who owns what, and what is happening around. If he doesn't know the answer he will soon find out. Can our people do the same here in Singapore? Are we equally resourceful or alert, I wonder? Isn't it about entrepreneurship, productivity, not giving up and speed?

Incidentally, he dressed immaculately well—nice suit and tie. When I first met him I was impressed. Polite and confident, he looked like a managing director to me! When you look good, you feel good, speak well and you can do good! I think it is our attitude and our outlook on life!

End Note

1 Anthony Seah was then the senior vice president (Projects) in Pidemco Land.

Liew Mun Leong/President & CEO **26/08/2002** 04:47 PM

To:	All Staff
cc:	Board of Directors
bcc:	

Subject: **Creativity Pays**

Cap/taLand

... Building People

S taff suggestions[1] are an important driving force to enable a company to be innovative and entrepreneurial. These suggestions should come from all levels of staff, as they know their jobs best.

We initiated a scheme for staff feedback, administered by PSET,[2] back in 1998. Staff were encouraged to give suggestions regarding maintenance and service standards in the buildings owned and managed by the CapitaLand group of companies, and PSET would then follow up with the relevant departments which would act upon them.

The number of suggestions continued to increase to around 100 a month and the scope was enlarged in mid-2001

to include suggestions that will:
- create new business opportunities;
- generate additional revenues;
- save operational costs;
- improve our corporate image; and
- improve our service standards, etc.

These suggestions are important to our business growth. We value them and we encourage more staff to participate. So far, the contributions have come mainly from PREMAS International.[3] Other strategic business units (SBU) account for only 20% of total submissions.

The percentage of innovative ideas remains at around 10% of the feedback received. We want to encourage all staff to put on their thinking caps and come forward with more innovative ideas that are related to our business.

In the last staff communication session, I announced that:
- the top contributor of PSET feedback will be considered to be in the Global Learning Team, which will visit world-class, leading companies in advanced countries, and
- we will give S$500 (US$300) for good suggestions.

In addition to the above, I have also informed the CEOs in each SBU to reward good suggestions with up to S$1,000.

All these aim to stimulate your creative thinking. So, log on to the PSET feedback form and make your suggestions.

I wish you all the best in your submissions.

Postscript: The scheme was terminated in 2005 when PREMAS International was divested. In 2006, CapitaLand introduced another incentive scheme, ICE (Innovation, Creativity, Entrepreneurship).

End Notes

1 Liew Mun Leong started encouraging staff to think creatively as early as 1998. An electronic staff feedback scheme was then implemented as an avenue for staff to point out lapses in service and to give suggestions.
2 PSET stands for Property Services Enhancement Team.
3 PREMAS International was the property services arm of CapitaLand.

Liew Mun Leong/President & CEO **05/06/2006** 02:09 PM

To: All Staff

cc: Board of Directors

bcc:

Subject: **Who Stole Our Cheese?**

CapitaLand

... Building People

A fter a long weekend's grief over losing the Marina Bay IR bid,[1] I kept asking myself the question: "Why did we lose?"

I went jogging yesterday morning and reflected on this painful question again. The answer struck me. It is what the hospitality industry calls MICE (meetings, incentives, conventions and exhibitions), and from now onwards MICE will remain in my mind as our corporate lesson to remember.

THIS CORPORATE CREATURE IS DANGEROUS

At the subsequent staff communication session yesterday I

spoke about why we lost the Marina Bay IR bid and the lessons learnt. The message is so important that I think it is worth repeating here some of the key discussion points for those who were unable to attend the session and for our overseas colleagues.

PAINFUL ACCEPTANCE

It is grossly disappointing and painful, but we have to accept that we were defeated. The team worked very hard, but the verdict is out. I repeatedly stressed that we must accept and respect the government's decision. In business we say "the customer is always right". We must never bad mouth the customer, the winner or our colleagues who have worked assiduously on the project. I would take a serious view of any colleague who behaves as a bad loser, unhelpfully "throwing stones" now at the customer, the competitor or ourselves.

THE MOST INTENSIVE COMPETITION

The Marina Bay IR bid is what I would call the "mother of all competitions". Building six million sq ft (557,418 sq m) at a cost of S$5 billion (US$3.2 billion) is easily Singapore's largest project, attracting all the top gaming resort players in the world. It will have a significant economic, social and political impact. The Ministry of Trade and Industry claims that it could contribute S$2.7 billion to GDP and create 30,000 jobs. It is Singapore's most talked about project in recent times.

DID WE PUT UP A STRONG COMPETITIVE TEAM?

CapitaLand is known to be one of the largest quality developers in Singapore and with the most international development experience. All the big gaming companies, including the eventual winner, had approached us to be their partner. It was management's unanimous decision to partner MGM. It is the largest gaming resort player in Las Vegas, and in our assessment, we share similar corporate values and culture. MGM's highly qualified and successful top management team operates very corporately and is well-regarded by both the gaming community and the Las Vegas authorities. We employed top-notch architects in the US in the design preparation. But, alas, we were on the wrong track.

SO WHY DID WE LOSE THE BID?

We had put up the best team effort possible, but the verdict is that someone else was seen by the customer as being better. During my national service days, I was taught that "doing our best" is not good enough—how true!

SOME OF MY ANALYSIS ON OUR FAILURE:

(a) Sands is prepared to put in much more money than we were—an estimated S$1 billion more. They were the highest bidder. Based on our financial feasibility study, we couldn't afford this budget.

(b) Sands read the customer's needs accurately. The Singapore Tourism Board targets to have an additional two million sq ft of MICE space by 2015. Sands offered them 1.5 million sq ft by 2010. Our proposal was only 400,000 sq ft based on the fact that the current Singapore Expo is only 20% occupied. We focused on entertainment, retail and F&B instead of MICE. We made the killer mistake of not identifying MICE as the customer's wish to achieve its strategic goal. Whether logical or not, we forgot that the customer is always right.

ARCHITECTURE

This is very subjective and there is no point debating on this subject now. There are always some pluses and minuses to any design-form or circulation, simplicity, etc. Some designs grow on us, e.g., the "durian"[1] was strongly criticised by the public, but now it seems quite lovable to the original critics, including me!

LESSONS LEARNT

(a) We didn't do our marketing study right. We failed to spot the customer's wish!

(b) The joint-venture was very strong corporately in terms of systems, structure and culture, and we did our analysis and sums logically, which impaired our entrepreneurial vision. Yes, we have to clear financial hurdles of IRR[2] in our financial feasibility study, but we also have to weigh that against the rare opportunity that the project presented, and the chance to gain track record. From the shareholders' perspective, what Sands has to invest additionally, and bullishly, now may be offset commercially by the immediate share price gains. It was single-minded, extremely focused on what its customers wanted and entrepreneurial about the business prospects and the total financial gains. I am not saying that we do not have all these, but it's obvious Sands' approach was more enterprising and bolder than ours.

(d) Maybe as a large corporation we also had a distorted image of who was driving our show. Even in our presentations, we had too many "cooks". Perhaps we should have had one "father of the product"—one "star driver".

(e) We identified and focused on the wrong competitor. Yes, Harrah's/Keppel was strong, but we completely missed out and underestimated the "dark horse"—Sands.

(f) We did not fully mobilise our total in-house capability and expertise—i.e., we have lots of experts and experience in retail, F&B, and hospitality in the group to harness.

So what's next? We have paid the price in our first major defeat. We have to make it back. No use crying over spilt milk and don't spend energy blaming, grieving and smarting over it. We will go for the Sentosa bid now. This round, it will be

... a CapitaLand Commercial and Integrated Development effort, but a "CapitaLand Group Project". We have to put the best team forward and mobilise everyone to contribute to the effort.

MICE AS OUR CORPORATE LESSON

(a) MICE in its different forms is an insidious corporate enemy.

(b) It is hidden and secretive, yet cannot be totally eliminated as it will surface in different ways. There will always be MICE in our business.

(c) Identify them early and act fast on them. One cannot pretend they don't exist just because we can't see them.

So the final lesson is: Who and where are the MICE in our business or project. How do we deal with them? Use a big mousetrap.

If we are blind to this threat, it will again quietly and insidiously steal our cheese (or bacon) away.

Whilst this is a painful episode for us, we must learn to laugh at our adversity and go forward to our next opportunity. We should take heart from the wise words of our chairman, Richard Hu: "Please convey to the Marina IR team my congratulations for putting up a great bid. I had every confidence that we would succeed, but the customer is always right and we must accept the outcome and move on. There are many other worlds to conquer!"

End Notes

1 In 2005, CapitaLand teamed up with MGM Mirage to bid for the rights to develop Singapore's first integrated resort (IR) in Marina Bay, but it lost out to Las Vegas Sands Corporation in May 2006.

2 Esplanade – Theatres on the Bay in Singapore is one of the world's busiest arts centres, officially opened on 12 October 2002. An architectural icon, Singaporeans fondly called it "durian", alluding to its distinctive twin shells which resemble the fruit.

3 IRR refers to an investment's internal rate of return.

Liew Mun Leong/President & CEO **27/11/2006** 05:31 PM

To:	All Staff
cc:	Board of Directors
bcc:	

Cap/taLand

Subject: **Catching MICE with ICE—**
CapitaLand's New Corporate Culture

... Building People

L ast Tuesday at our sixth anniversary staff communication session, (webcasted to our colleagues all around the world) I spoke about creating a new corporate culture in CapitaLand. I named this new movement "ICE", which stands for Innovation, Creativity and Entrepreneurship.

This is such an important group-wide initiative that I will be writing a series of emails to explain and market the whole concept to each and every one of the 7,600 colleagues in CapitaLand.

This is the first in the series.

BACKGROUND- WHY ICE NOW?

A few months ago, at a management retreat, I suggested that we brainstorm how we can remain competitively ahead of the market. In essence, most of the ideas presented revolved around being innovative, creative and entrepreneurial. In my concluding speech I put forward the idea that we should start an ICE movement and thereafter instructed corporate planning to plan for the birth of ICE.

How important is ICE? Currently there is a strong market for real estate business across Asia Pacific, the Middle East and Russia for us to take. We have done many outstanding real estate projects in the region and have chalked up a good track record and reputation. We have developed, across all real estate sectors, strong domain knowledge, equally impressive financial engineering skills, a robust balance sheet and a deep-enough management bench to be a credible player anywhere. To me, we need one more winning factor to embrace all the existing elements in our "value chain"—ICE.

So:
Market + Real Estate Domain Knowledge + Management Bench + Balance Sheet + ICE = Market Winner

ICE AS CHANGE AGENT

Due to globalisation, we all know that changes in the market will be much more aggressive and faster. New products, processes and industry inflection points will make us outdated if we don't understand and address the forces of change. We will become irrelevant and be outdone by others. How shall we cope with globalisation if we can't change fast enough?

ICE, ICE, ICE FOR EVERYONE

Innovation is being championed by everyone, everywhere. Chinese leaders and officials I meet do not talk about more investments, but about innovation. The chairman of the China Security Commission spoke at the World Economic Forum recently, stressing that the financial and capital markets in China need more innovation rather than more investments. So do the political leaders. Japan's new prime minister, in one of his maiden speeches, also spoke about innovation in addition to technology *per se.* Singapore's Senior Minister Goh Chok Tong is now in Italy forging links for a master's degree course that is a collaboration between Nanyang Technological University and Milan's top design school, Domus Academy (reputed as one of the top three in the world in its field). The CEOs of two of the world's largest conglomerates, Proctor & Gamble and General Electric (GE), are actively championing innovation and creativity in their organisations, and they are winning in their performances. ICE is competitive survival for people, companies and countries.

ICE, OUR NEW CORPORATE CULTURE

ICE must be inculcated into our corporate culture almost as a new DNA for us. It should permeate all levels of our organisation, so much so that it becomes our natural habit to think and act in "ICE-y" ways. It will not work with just preaching from me at a staff communication session and then with several emails. It must not be a fad that comes and goes. To be frank, some companies practise their QCC[1] programme that way and it flops. Call it DNA, in our blood, or just plain habit, but we must think the ICE way!

ICE—PROCESSES, PRODUCTS AND BUSINESS IDEAS

ICE must cover all areas of change—Processes, Products and most importantly, Business Ideas. To illustrate the point, I will use an example from the book *What's the Big Idea* by Thomas Davenport and Laurence Prusak comparing the performance of Westinghouse and GE. Both groups have been competing with each other since the late nineteenth century for a leadership position in the industrial world. Westinghouse used pride itself on lots of innovative technological inventions, whilst GE hit it big with business ideas in addition to its R&D programme. Westinghouse has now disintegrated and its businesses have been dismantled and divested as a result of poor financial performances. GE has relentlessly delivered more than 20% annual growth to its shareholders, making it one of the most valuable companies in the world. In addition to its technological prowess, it promotes innovative business and management improvement ideas aggressively across the group, be it globalisation (one of the first US companies to truly globalise), Six Sigma, embrace e-commerce, be No. 1, 2 or 3 in the business, vitality curve, etc.

"Who stole our cheese? MICE!"
"How do we steal it back? ICE!"

End Note

1 QCC stands for Quality Control Circle, a small group of workers (6-10 persons) from the same work unit who meet regularly to identify, select and analyse work-related problems so that they can make suggested solutions to management.

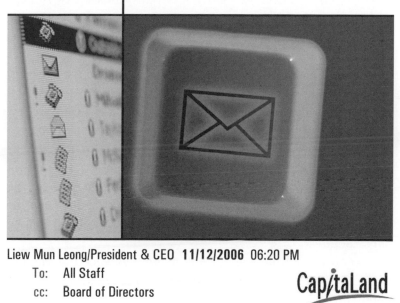

Liew Mun Leong/President & CEO **11/12/2006** 06:20 PM

To: All Staff

cc: Board of Directors

bcc:

Subject: **Winning with Ideas**

Cap/taLand

... Building People

Last Friday was indeed an extremely stressful day for CapitaLand and for me. The morning saw the launch of our CapitaRetail China Trust (CRCT). Immediately at the strike of the gong at the Singapore Exchange, the unit price rose from S$1.13 (US$0.73) to S$1.60, ending the day at S$1.80— an almost 60% gain in capital value. When leaving the SGX[1], Hsuan Owyang, chairman of CRCT, told me, as though prophetically, that at the end of the day, "We will win some and lose some".

How true his philosophy in life proved to be, when by 5:15pm we got the very disappointing news that the winner of the Sentosa IR[2] was not to be us! From that moment, I was deluged with dozens of phone calls, SMSes and emails from friends, partners, well-wishers, colleagues and some from overseas and board members offering comforting words of support and encouragement. Some were words of agitation with the client's decision, but I was really heartened to hear their loud rally behind us. One was from a young colleague who joined us only two months ago, pledging her pride in the company and urging me to keep the spirits high.

I thanked all of them but rationalised that the decision belongs to the client, no matter how good our proposal was. I have also spoken and written to Sol Kerzner and Frank Gehry, and we are of one mind that we should not let our effort go to waste. I felt particularly bad for Frank since as a superstar architect he is not known to have to compete for his design, but that world-class developers have to court him, most of the time in futility. He is highly selective, but he decided that he would create an iconic design in Asia, and I was elated that he chose Sentosa.

Even though he was let down, he was sporting enough to comfort me and said he would go with us again at the next opportunity in Asia.

The strong team spirit and commitment of these two world-class creative and entrepreneurial talents to work with us again were gratifying. Even though the prize went to someone else, we have learnt so much from both of these geniuses during the bidding preparation process. The efforts and lessons are rewarding in themselves.

So what happened?

First, let's face it: the battle was between Universal theme park and us. Clearly, watching the TV interviews last night, the members of the public were all talking about how happy they were about Universal coming to town. Ditto the local papers yesterday and today. They talked about not having to fly to Los Angeles or Osaka to enjoy a Universal theme park. Universal is a world-renowned resort, and though we have the world's top architecture guru Frank Gehry to produce a most stunning design, and Kerzner with the world's largest aquasphere filled with robotic sea creatures swimming next to thousands of the real stuff, we were not able to pitch successfully to the client, who felt that Universal was a "tried-and-tested" brand.

We knew early on when our competitor roped in Universal that we would have a tough fight no matter how weak we may have perceived that competitor to be. After much persuasion, Sol Kerzner managed to bring Frank Gehry on board and we further reinforced our product's creativity with robotics experts from MIT and new experience creator Peter Arnell to package a highly creative "out-of-the-box" product so that we could "blow the customers away". Sol had successfully developed frontier gaming resorts in South Africa, the Bahamas and Connecticut, US, which have successfully transformed the tourism economy in their respective areas. We had the right formula and we were highly confident of the outcome. I rated our proposal irresistible and undeniably the ultimate in resort design. But our competitor had a very strong "weapon" called Universal—a family theme park that is well-established and has been "selling fun" as a family attraction for a long time. It is also said that the Singapore Tourism Board has been courting Universal for a long time.

So the lesson is that no matter how we size up our competitors, don't underestimate what "weapon" they can procure to compete with us. As an analogy, who really took notice of emerging North Korea or Iran (except for the oil supplies and reserves) until they both threatened the world with their nuclear weapon programmes? The whole world was rattled!

Now that the IR chapter in Singapore is closed, there is no point smarting over it and asking why it went the other way.

What's next? As you are aware, all our other businesses are performing at top gear all over Asia Pacific and Europe. Recently we have also been aggressively exploring to move into the Gulf Co-operation Council region, Russia and also Kazakhstan. Opportunities are abundant. But we must still continue to develop our ILEC[3] business opportunities. On the very same day we found out about our miss in

Singapore, we also activated our marketing contacts to explore opportunities in China and India. Perhaps also in Thailand or Japan?

My final thought is that it is sometimes not enough to focus only on the products and processes, as I pointed out in the last staff meeting.

It is also about the business idea. With one masterly stroke of signing a contract with Universal, the IR prize was snatched away. But one truth remains: we have developed a highly creative "out-of-the-box" resort product. It is a stunning, unique product and no one could have done better here. We are very proud of our association with Kerzner and Gehry and of all the effort by everyone in the team.

Competition is the essence of business and we have to accept the outcome of the competition. That is, recognise the reality of business and move forward. Let's see.

End Notes

1 SGX is the Singapore Exchange.
2 In 2005, CapitaLand teamed up with Kerzner International to bid for the second licence up for grabs, to build an Integrated Resort (IR) on Sentosa Island. It enlisted famed architect Frank Gehry to design a futuristic resort. The joint-venture lost the bid to Genting International which had secured Universal Studios as the main anchor of its project.
3 ILEC – Integrated Leisure, Entertainment and Conventions.

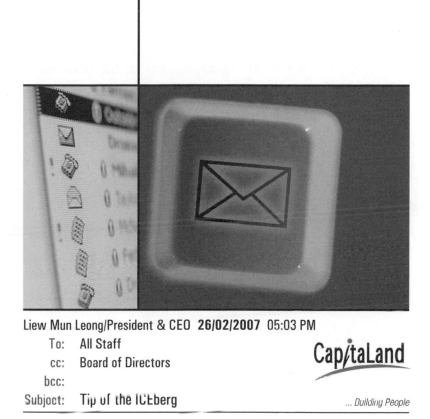

Liew Mun Leong/President & CEO **26/02/2007** 05:03 PM

To:	All Staff
cc:	Board of Directors
bcc:	

Subject: Tip of the ICEberg

Cap/taLand

... Building People

Recently, I joined the participants of CapitaLand's inaugural ICE Camp and its first ICE initiative. The three day/two-night camp was held at Changi Village Hotel with 34 people participating; they represented each strategic business unit (SBU) and several flew in from China, Japan, Thailand and Australia to attend.

The objectives of the ICE Camp were to build awareness of ICE and our ICE programme, provide participants with the tools to create and assess opportunities, and for people to have lots of fun. Fun is a very important part of ICE! I saw them having real fun, building a strong team in the process.

Unfortunately, I was unable to attend the entire camp, but the feedback and ideas suggested by the pioneering batch left me very encouraged that we can imbue CapitaLand's DNA with ICE.

At ICE Camp, I briefly spoke about what the elements of ICE mean to me:

- Innovation: process of implementing ideas for improvement;
- Creativity: idea generation, lateral and out-of-the-box thinking;
- Entrepreneurship: execution, taking the innovation to market.

I also stressed the importance of both big AND small ideas; I can tell you that my ideas have always started small and have grown from there. Many discoveries start small—Newton saw the falling apple and discovered/recognised/developed the law of gravity.

ICEBERG

The next step is to launch the second initiative, which is called ICEberg. ICEberg is the name of a newly-established channel where you can all direct your ideas and be rewarded for it (via the ICE Bucket—I will touch on this soon). The idea can be big or small. It can pertain to the group as a whole, a particular SBU, or a functional area. It can cover products, services, processes, business models or management practices—anything that can improve our performance. If you think it is a good idea, tell us about it! It is crucial that you speak out and articulate your ideas. Nothing is trivial or silly!

Why the name ICEberg?

- Ideas are the tip of the iceberg; they represent the potential for something huge, and beneath the surface lies an ICE culture that supports the visible tip and makes it rise above the waterline.

ICEBERG AND ICE BUCKET – HOW DO THEY WORK?

1) Ideas can be submitted to a special email account. If you are making a team submission, please appoint a team leader to liaise with the ICE team. ICE funds will be fairly distributed.

2) You will be informed via email when the ICE team retrieves your idea.

3) Your idea will be graded by the chief corporate officer and SBU CEOs or their nominees. You will be informed via email when your grade is finalised. This is likely to take a few weeks.

4) For each idea you submit, we will put S$25 (US$16.60) into the quarterly ICE Bucket (the more ideas, the more money in the ICE Bucket, although it will be capped at S$25,000 per quarter). The ICE Bucket will be distributed according to how well your idea scores.

5) If an idea results in financial gains, CapitaLand may reward you (the idea owner) above/beyond/in addition to the ICE Bucket earnings. The ICE team may also ask you to help further conceptualise your brilliant idea if such action is required.

WHAT IS A GOOD IDEA?

Panellists will consider the following when grading your idea:
• Originality;
• Potential to add value;
• Feasibility;
• Strategic fit.

I urge you to constantly question, and to act upon your ideas—big and small—either by creating the opportunity yourself or by submitting them to ICEberg.

I must tell you that it is my ICE-like attitude that has gotten me where I am today. Nothing is too small or too big.

I believe that this ICE movement will be crucial to differentiate CapitaLand from the rest in this competitive world. Be ICE-like, join us and have fun!

Chapter 3

Day-to-Day Business – Success is in the Details

"Every piece of execution is you. Shame on you if carelessness and wrong answers are branded on you."

C orporate discipline must rule the day-to-day operations of a business, but it is also very important for a CEO to keep an eye on details, from cutting red tape to making sure customers' queries are answered promptly.

I count myself as a hands-on CEO. While I like to empower employees, give them responsibility that will test them to their limit, I've always thought that if you're not hands-on, you cannot manage properly. I just don't believe in desktop management, and I always prefer to keep more than just an overview. Whatever we do, we must ultimately be able to stay on top of the matter as "the buck stops with you".

That said, as a leader, you must also be able to delegate. As a company moves overseas, I do not believe it is possible to manage successfully from the "mother ship" located somewhere else—someone sitting far away can't really tell what's happening somewhere else, which is why choosing able country team leaders is so important.

I do not believe in leadership that is feeble or too accommodating. Strong leadership, albeit not a dictatorial one, means being decisive and accepting responsibility.

I stand by my own convictions and core value system. To be a good leader you need not only vision, but also the courage and conviction to carry through your vision. Too many leaders don't have that courage. You also need people skills and the ability to communicate, to inspire and to lead.

The same way that you can convey your core values through anecdotal stories, you can also convey important management and behavioural messages by pointing to simple examples people can relate to.

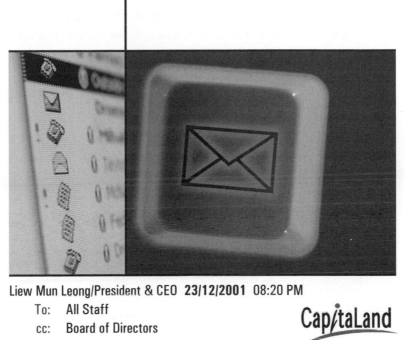

Liew Mun Leong/President & CEO **23/12/2001** 08:20 PM

To: All Staff

cc: Board of Directors

bcc:

Subject: **Osama Otak**

Cap/taLand

... Building People

I 'm not going to send one of those gimmicky electronic cards, but I will tell you an amusing personal story instead as a festive greeting.

Last week I went with a friend to a modest coffee shop in Katong to satisfy my yearning for chilli-hot *nasi padang*[1]. I had not been there for years. After I had ordered my big spread I heard someone shouting "Osama otak,[2] Osama otak". It looked like ordinary "otak", but still, the strange branding attracted my attention. Surprisingly, nearly everyone in the coffee shop was happily chomping them!

Were we missing out on something special? I was naturally tempted and asked for the price. The smart hawker proudly pushed a dozen to me with his convincing marketing tune "Osama otak, one dollar one". I bought four—two for each of us. We opened them and expected to uncover a new recipe. We were disappointed. No great shakes—just ordinary otak toasted hot on the charcoal stove, mischievously but loudly branded as "Osama otak"! Whatever it means, they were selling like hot cakes because customers bought them out of curiosity.

The next morning, I began to understand why he called them "Osama otak"—both my friend and I suffered.

Moral of the story:

(a) Don't get conned by branding that you don't understand.

(b) Don't take anything that you are unsure of into your system—be it your body (especially your stomach), home, company or country. Whatever may be the branding or story behind it, you may live to regret it!

Merry X'mas and a Happy New Year to you and your family. Oh, if anyone tries to sell you an Osama turkey, don't buy it, please! We want you back in the office quickly after the festive season.

End Notes

1 *Nasi padang* refers to Malay/Indonesian food; *nasi* means rice in the Malay language; Padang is located in West Sumatra, Indonesia.
2 Otak refers to a type of fish cake cooked in Malay style. It can be eaten as a snack or with bread or rice as part of a meal.

Liew Mun Leong/President & CEO **07/01/2002** 05:01 PM

To: All Staff

cc: Board of Directors

bcc:

Subject: Cultural Integration

Cap/taLand

... Building People

J ust before Christmas, we held a small tea reception where I gave away letters of promotion to some junior and middle management colleagues. It is a simple but nice gesture we used to practise in Pidemco Land to congratulate staff who had done well. At the reception, I spoke on several points:

(1) We will always look after our staff, especially those who have done well. They can be promoted every year and come back to this "promotion reception" year after year. In fact, some do. It is all about meritocratic rewards.

(2) Doing well yourself is not enough. We encourage teamwork as a key ingredient to one's potential. At the same time, we will watch your commitment to work for the good of the wider group interest. Can you work for the interest of CapitaLand as a group?

Do you ever think of it?

Promoting, or at least being able to work with, the post-merger integration will be a very important assessment of your performance. CapitaLand is now one company, one name and one management. Many mergers have crumbled because of failures in post-merger integration. Daimler-Chrysler, a US$36 billion "made-in-heaven" merger, is a classic case. It quickly turned into a "rocky marriage" because of continued polarisation between the German (Daimler) and the American (Chrysler) counterparts. "Marriage of equals" was their catch phrase and staff took it in that spirit. However, the cultures and corporate practices of the two companies were notoriously difficult to fuse together. One large shareholder who is on the board commented that by still calling it Daimler-Chrysler (with the hyphen between them) staff will continue to see it as two companies! Their share price dropped from a high of about US$80 to as low as US$40 as the company started to report losses in the third and fourth quarters of 2000.

It is easy to chant merger slogans. Making it work requires commitment. At CapitaLand, we will be promoting behaviour and conduct that support the integration process. Best practices will be adopted; shortcomings—wherever they are from—identified and improved. So far, I am happy to report that the integration progress has been going smoothly and this is encouraging.

See you at this year's tea reception!

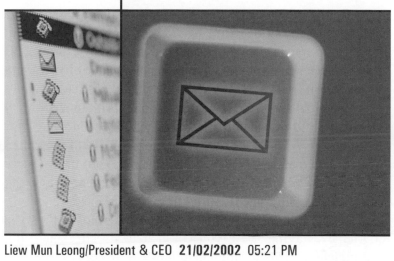

Liew Mun Leong/President & CEO **21/02/2002** 05:21 PM

To: All Staff

cc: Board of Directors

bcc:

Subject: **Don't Let Fertile Water Flow to Others' Fields（肥水不流外人田）**

CapitaLand

... Building People

C apitaLand owns more than 60% of Raffles Hotel group and more than 70% of Ascott group. Together they have more than 6,000 hotel rooms and serviced apartments in more than 20 cities in Asia Pacific and Europe. Raffles just acquired another hotel in Los Angeles and we intend to grow our hotel/ serviced apartment business further.

To me, it just makes pure business sense for us to stay in our own hotels/serviced apartments whenever possible.

(a) For every S$100 (US$ 57) spent on our hotel bills, we get S$60 or S$70 back into our revenue. As there is commonly a 5% to 10% vacancy rate (we do have 100% occupancy sometimes though), it will be marginal costing for us to take up the vacant rooms that are perishable in any case. So it will simply boost our revenue and profits if we make it a point to stay in our hotels/serviced apartments whenever possible.

(b) Patronising our facilities demonstrates our commitment and pride. If we don't trust our product quality and service, who will? Wouldn't you be proud to tell your business clients/associates that you are staying in CapitaLand's properties there? Or if you are on a private visit with your family or loved ones, show and tell them that your company owns or manages such magnificent hotels or serviced apartments. I have visited and stayed in many of them. They are excellent. So far, I haven't seen any bad ones—at least not yet.

(c) And by staying there you could help us check out any deficiencies in the product quality and service—be it a blown bulb, dirty towels, unsafe lifts or a rude receptionist. Our operators will take feedback positively and make necessary remedies and improvements.

(d) I have suggested to both Raffles and Ascott to work out "triple C" (corporate, corporate, corporate) rates for CapitaLand based on long-term commitments on a large volume basis. These rates mean savings for the whole group. This is another cost-saving proposal under our strategic cost management programme.

Richard Helfer and Kee Teck Koon, as CEOs of Raffles and Ascott respectively, are both working out the rates. There are various comfortable grades. Raffles has its own five-star luxurious class (e.g. Brown's Hotel in London) and four-star business class (e.g. Merchant Court in Sydney). Similarly, Ascott has its own range of four- and five-star serviced apartments, which I have stayed in and found very comfortable. They are like hotels except for the absence of

F&B and conference facilities. They are less formal and could be like a home away from home. If Ascott and Raffles are both available in the city you are staying in, you can take your pick.

I have proposed to management a company policy that staff must lodge in our hotels/serviced apartments whenever available. I spoke about it at the staff communication session last week, too. I suggest that we implement this policy with effect from March 15th.

CEOs and Human Resources, please obtain the details and rates from Raffles and Ascott next week. Anthony Seah, please get Synergistic Cost Management Division to measure the results. We will agree to exceptions only when there are certain operational reasons such as the following:

(i) Inconveniences because the meetings/conventions are held somewhere distant from our facilities.

(ii) Our facilities are very remote from our other business meetings and will induce delays and additional travelling cost.

(iii) You are obliged, out of courtesy, to stay where your other business associates are staying. Mind you, this is going to be difficult to prove!

(iv) There are other much cheaper hotels and serviced apartments compared to our "triple C" rates—in which case Raffles and Ascott will have to tell me why we are not competitive.

Oh yes, there is one more exception to staying in hotels/serviced apartments that we don't own or manage. This is when we are looking at a prospective candidate for acquisition or to take over its management, or investigating a very successful competitor who is hurting us. Then it is prudent to check out why they succeed or fail, their operations, management, and location, etc.

But then you don't have to stay there too many times to check out such strengths or weaknesses, unless you are doing what in engineering we call a "fatigue test". This is subjecting a material to stress until it fails—like bending a wire to-and-fro until it breaks!

I have said before (and I meant it) that if staff fail to see the wider interest of the group and continue to stay outside our list of properties without cogent reasons as mentioned above, they will have to pick up their own bills. (Finance Department, please note this instruction for implementation.)

Staff can also use the "triple C" special rates when they are on private visits with their families. They must of course settle their own bills.

It is a win-win scheme. Where we should stay is the prerogative of the company as we are paying the bills. I have stayed in our facilities many times and I assure you that they are as good as any comparable class in town. We could take a tip from the Japanese, as Japanese companies are very cohesive and re-channel business back to their own subsidiaries or associate companies. No questioning and no need for policy—it's just considered a natural/moral obligation.

Operating in more than 32 cities, we are now a global company with a sizeable overseas lodging budget. Our lodging expenses are no small beer. Why not re-channel it back to the group? There is a Chinese saying, "Don't let fertile water flow to others' fields" (肥水不流外人田).

Happy staying at Raffles or Ascott!

Liew Mun Leong/President & CEO **15/04/2002** 05:28 PM

   To: All Staff

   cc: Board of Directors

   bcc:

Subject. **Cost-cutting Ideas**

CapitaLand

... Building People

R ecently, I sent an email to all strategic business unit (SBU) CEOs to cut operational costs by 5%.

Currently, many other CEOs around the world have successfully turned around their business performances by drastically cutting costs. You can read their success stories in many business magazines.

Last year, we started the synergistic cost management division (SCMD) to identify and coordinate cost savings across SBUs. For the year 2001, SCMD recorded a savings of S$36 million (US$19.7 million), which is a good start for our first operational year. This year, SCMD's target is S$50 million.

I am happy with these efforts as they have extended cost savings to many new areas—procurement of construction contracts, capital equipment, office materials, insurance, travel, accommodation, etc. Much of the initial scepticism and misgivings about synergistic cost savings across SBUs have been clarified and people have been won over. I am pleased to see the close co-operation between various purchasers of goods and services. They have even initiated new projects for SCMD to work on.

I have challenged SCMD to think of more major cost-saving items—to think "out of the box" and consider major items that may result in saving a few hundred thousands of dollars or even millions of dollars. The CEOs are cracking their heads on how to find major savings opportunities. The target is to save another 5% of their operational costs.

Some simple ideas—I read that the BBC has stopped serving cookies to go along with their coffee or tea. That saved them more than US$400,000 a year! PREMAS is promoting the idea of bulk energy purchases, which can save millions of dollars. At Raffles City alone we could save more than S$1 million a year if we did bulk energy purchases.

Staff can positively contribute cost-saving ideas in their operations. In a down market, we may not be able to increase our revenue significantly due to the negative economic climate. Reducing cost, on the other hand, is a much more controllable alternative to improve our bottom line. Of course, we must do both.

No ideas? Just look around and be sensitive about your costs when you are doing your work. Every cent counts, but it should also be the right corporate discipline to inculcate within CapitaLand.

When Queen Elizabeth II advertised recently to recruit a Keeper of the Privy Purse, she insisted that experience in cost-cutting was a plus. The former Keeper "had double-glazed windows installed to reduce heating bills, eliminated the footmen's beer subsidy and used cheaper marquees for her garden parties". The queen did her part, too, roaming the corridors of Buckingham Palace, switching off unneeded lights. How about you? If the queen can do it, we can too.

Liew Mun Leong/President & CEO **18/05/2002** 04:30 PM

   To: All Staff

   cc: Board of Directors

  bcc:

Subject: **Knock-out Kaya Toast**

Cap/taLand

... Building People

A simple fierce competition story here.

This morning, after my medical appointment at Raffles Hospital (CapitaLand owns half the building, not the hospital), I went down to the cafeteria for coffee. A charming and tasteful environment, no less than the best cafeteria in town. I bought a cup of coffee for 90 cents (US$0.51) from a stall. At a normal hawker centre, it would cost 60 or 70 cents.

As I was sipping my condensed milk coffee, I noticed that many people around me were happily buying their coffee in a plastic tray that came with two half-boiled eggs and a slice of nicely toasted *kaya*[1] *roti*.[2] A boy at the next table loudly cracked his two eggs and out popped the soft-boiled yolks and whites. I looked around and saw something that made me feel stupid (and actually quite angry). A large marketing board (which I had missed) put up by the same stall I bought my coffee from was loudly marketing a promotion set:

2 half-boiled eggs + 1 toasted kaya bread + coffee = all for only $1!!!

It is ridiculous! I could have paid just 10 cents more to get two eggs and a piece of kaya bread—a full breakfast!

Guess what I saw next? Something even more ridiculous! Just less than 10 metres away in the same cafeteria, there was a famous, original "Ya Kun" outlet with its specially designed and franchised theme. Ya Kun (started in 1944 as a humble coffee stall) is an old favourite with many Singaporeans for the traditional coffee stall's half-boiled eggs and kaya toast. It now has franchised operations in many locations. They have gone up-market and operate in more luxurious locations. In this Raffles Hospital Ya Kun outlet, you have to pay S$3.30 for the same set of items! The coffee stall that I sat at was trying to "corner" Ya Kun by ridiculously charging less than one third of the price for a similar meal that Ya Kun is famous for! Not so-friendly neighbours, apparently.

Some simple questions:

(a) No matter how great Ya Kun's toast or how yummy its kaya, would you pay three times more? Bear in mind—this is not a high-class, branded product (or dining) where there is more room for differentiation. Just kaya roti with half-boiled eggs and coffee! Have they overpriced themselves or has someone underpriced mindlessly to hijack the business?

(b) Shouldn't they have told me that by paying 10 cents more I could have a full breakfast? Of course, the margin of selling just a cup coffee is so much greater than the breakfast set, so why should they? But as a customer I felt cheated. Was it the right thing to do?

(c) How does the coffee stall manage the costs to sell at one third of Ya Kun's? Bread, eggs, coffee, and condensed milk are all commodity items, so how much cheaper can you get them from vendors? I suppose they have to pay similar rental rates.

(d) Is he just trying to break even or get the contribution from his business volume? He sells other miscellaneous coffee stall items too.

(e) Will he increase his price later?

(f) How long will the competition last? Who will blink first?

This is the nature of business nowadays. Your very neighbour may try to "kill" (or is it to skin?) you with unbelievable pricing.

What do you do? Although there were still some customers in the Ya Kun shop, the coffee stall that was under-cutting was visibly getting more customers at the time I was there.

Where do we go from here, when your immediate neighbour is out to "destroy" your pricing? Let's watch this simple price war over kaya roti and see if there are some corporate lessons to learn.

If there is nothing you can learn from this email, at least you now know where to get a S$1 breakfast in a nice cafeteria!

End Notes

1 Kaya (means "rich" in Malay, based on its golden colour) is a jam made from coconut milk and duck or chicken eggs, which is flavoured with pandan leaves and sweetened with sugar.
2 Roti is the Hindi, Urdu, Punjabi, Pashto, Indonesian, Malaysian, Bengali word for bread.

Liew Mun Leong/President & CEO **08/09/2002** 05:25 PM

To: All Staff

cc: Board of Directors

bcc:

Subject: **Handling Difficult Customers**

Cap/taLand

... Building People

W hy do some Singaporeans turn ugly—newly acquired wealth, power, status and/or "sophistication"?

I met one on my return trip from Shanghai to Singapore. Standing in front of me at the check-in counter, this middle-aged Chinese man was causing a small commotion in Mandarin. He was having difficulty with a card box (about 20cm square and 1.5m tall) that he was carrying and it took an unduly long time to clear him. He protested angrily to the check-in staff.

Inside the aircraft he was again complaining loudly at the Singapore Airlines (SIA) staff who were trying to store his precious box. He was shouting that they had to solve his storage problem and that there was expensive stuff in the plain-looking box. He demanded the names of the two SIA staff who couldn't please him with their repeated attempts to store his "precious" box, and threatened that he would make an official complaint against them.

A calm-looking senior steward came to the rescue. He gently took the box to the clothes closet and attempted to place it vertically inside. The complaining passenger did not relent and again started screaming. The senior steward kept silent and tolerated the scolding. But our friend was not appeased and got high with his torrent of hard-hitting words. Then came what I thought was the ultimate insult—he said they were all "*ben dan*" (笨蛋) meaning "dumb eggs" in Mandarin. This is one of the worst and most degrading ways to call someone stupid. And he repeated this condemnation twice to them!

I was sitting near the clothes closet and witnessed this public humiliation of the SIA staff. I was upset by this unreasonable behaviour and intended to intervene, but the senior steward handled it very carefully and with dignity. He gently told this ugly passenger in Mandarin that they were already trying very hard to accommodate his awkward-sized box and said, "but please don't scold us this way". I could see that he was swallowing his pride and was badly humiliated. But he kept his cool. I was afraid that he would retaliate with some rude response or even with a punch because being called "dumb egg" in public is very infuriating. If I were in his position, I'm not sure I could restrain myself!

The passenger went back to his seat still smarting from his dissatisfaction, albeit in a lower tone. Some ugly foreigner that we had to tolerate to make a living, I thought. I subsequently caught sight of his red Singapore passport. He was a Singaporean! I was appalled and, frankly, was embarrassed by this Singaporean's behaviour.

When the plane landed, the senior steward took the box to the passenger as though nothing had happened. He even said goodbye and thanked his difficult passenger when he left the aircraft. Gracious service crew!

Customer lessons:

(i) If you are the customer, please don't be ugly even though you have paid a lot for the service;

(ii) In the service industry we will come across all sorts of unreasonable and difficult people; and

(iii) What do we do and how do we handle such a crisis? Remember that we are being watched in public, how we handle such a crisis. Stay calm, remain cool and on top of the situation. Being able to handle such tricky situations is what will distinguish us from the others.

But please don't be an ugly Singaporean—here or anywhere, anytime!

Liew Mun Leong/President & CEO **03/07/2003** 08:37 PM

    To: All Staff
    cc: Board of Directors
   bcc:
Subject: **Customer Urgency**

Cap/taLand

... Building People

R ecently I received several complaints from some of our customers (mainly retail/office tenants, hotels and serviced residences guests, and our residential home buyers) that we are not replying to their inquiries/requests fast enough. There are cases of our retail and office tenants asking for rental reviews/rebates or potential tenants competing for retail space at our popular malls. There are also complaints from our housing buyers on defects and requests for remedial works. They eventually resort to writing nasty letters or emails to me threatening legal action on the company.

We may be troubled with their requests—a request for rental reduction is not easy to deal with—but we must make the decision fast and reply to them quickly and officially, either in emails or letters. There is no point in delaying telling customers negative news just because they will not like to hear it, or in giving them hazy answers.

Sometimes I am told our colleagues "spoke" to them, but the customer can still turn around to complain that we have not replied "officially" to them—i.e. in writing.

We must handle customers professionally and efficiently. Get the answer from the company fast and reply to them firmly and officially—a definitive yes or no and alternative solutions, if any.

Times are hard and our clients can go away any time. In bad times or good times we must be seen to be efficient and effective in dealing with our customers.

We can talk to our customers, but we must also learn the habit of REPLYING TO THEM FAST AND IN WRITING to avoid any misunderstanding!

Liew Mun Leong/President & CEO **25/07/2005** 06:35 PM

To: All Staff

cc: Board of Directors

bcc:

Subject: **Shareholders Invest Money in Us, not Emotions**

CapitaLand

... Building People

W hy did we agree to sell the Raffles Hotel business?[1] It is the biggest divestment exercise in the CapitaLand group, which will change the landscape of the hospitality industry in Singapore. Let me give you some background so that you can understand and appreciate this transaction better.

First, let me clarify that that was a Raffles Holdings Ltd (RHL) transaction and full credit should be accorded to RHL. Management at RHL is always on the lookout for ways to unlock shareholders' value and it found a very profitable exit strategy. As a major shareholder, we saw that this made complete business sense. The board of RHL accepted the management's recommendation and CapitaLand as a major shareholder agreed to vote in favour of it.

CORPORATE BACKGROUND

We became a major shareholder of Raffles Holdings Ltd in late 2000 as a consequence of Pidemco Land's merger with DBS Land. At that time, we had in our fold four hotels, built and owned under Pidemco Land. They were the Equatorial in Yangon, Meritus West Lake in Hanoi, Sheraton in Suzhou and Four Seasons in London's Canary Wharf. Whilst we were the owner of these wonderfully built hotels (we built them), we had never managed them.

During the course of the merger, we were often asked by analysts and the investment community whether we would divest our stake in Raffles Holdings. It was quite a difficult call as then the share price was dismally low, trading at 47.5 cents per share versus the 1999 IPO price of 85 cents per share.

Divesting would mean incurring a huge paper loss even before we could start business. We took six months to develop and conclude the strategic intent of our hospitality business, which included Raffles and Ascott. We finally decided to "roll up our sleeves" to help build up both hospitality groups.

BUILDING VALUE AT RAFFLES

It has not been easy for Raffles to build up its value amidst the adverse economic environment caused by the Iraq war, SARS[2] and a general economic downturn. But we made some hard decisions on reorganisation and injected new managerial and leadership talent, pared down costs, set financial targets to management, diversified our geographic spread by expanding into Europe and US through the acquisition of the Swissotel chain (which saved the day in Asia during the SARS period), divested low-yielding or loss-making assets, and adopted an asset-light strategy by winning more management contracts. It worked. The financial performances speak for themselves.

Raffles management deserves full credit and compliments on making the effort and changes.

CAN WE GROW THE HOTEL BUSINESS FURTHER OURSELVES?

Today, in terms of room inventory and market-capital size, we are in 17th or 18th position in the world. We have 12,000 rooms whilst the biggest hotel group, Cendant, has 540,000 rooms, 45 times our size. Our market cap is US$573 million, against Cendant's US$25.38 billion—they are again more than 40 times bigger than us. In the hotel business you need some critical scale to compete internationally, and to put ourselves in, say, the 10th position, we would need something like another S$2 billion (US$1.18 billion) to be pumped in. Could we afford it and how long would it have taken to build up to this size?

WHY SELL IT NOW?

So for some time now, Raffles' management has been studying how to "unlock value" for shareholders. In the meantime, as the hotel business was improving globally, several offers were made to us to divest the business. They were not particularly attractive but these offers spurred the management to look into the divestment more seriously. To get the best deal, Raffles management commissioned a reputable investment bank to do further market study and to facilitate the transaction, if any. Bidding was very competitive and after two months of intense negotiations, the best offer emerged. The rest is now history.

WHAT ABOUT SENTIMENT AND EMOTION?

Putting aside the obvious economic value of the deal, I have been asked by journalists and many others about the sentimental value of Raffles Hotel. I made three points:

(1) As a business, particularly as a publicly listed company, we cannot make business investment or divestment decisions

based on sentimental values or emotions. This transaction would make a profit of S$605 million. We would indeed be irresponsible towards our shareholders if we had chosen to forgo this huge gain. At its current rate of growth, it could easily take the company 12 years or more to realise this kind of gain, not forgetting that there is absolutely no guarantee that the gains could indeed be achieved year after year. Others with stronger networking and financial strength may take a shorter time, but not us as we are now. Remember, the hotel business can be very volatile.

(2) Even if we allow ourselves to dwell on emotions, a change of ownership at Raffles Hotel will not change its history and legacy. The building's status is protected under the Preservation of Monument Act and the new owner is legally bound not to change its character. And after all, they have paid a handsome sum for it; it will be as much in their interest to ensure that the hotel is not run down. The British sold Harrods to an Egyptian-born businessman and the Americans sold Rockefeller Center to a Japanese group. Has anything happened to these two iconic buildings? They are still standing untouched in London and New York, respectively. Several Singapore groups including government-linked companies have acquired well-known or iconic buildings all over the world, including hotels in the US, Japan, Australia and Korea. They are still just as grand now.

(3) Singapore is a free economy. The capital market and stock market must be open to all. Similarly, commercial assets must always be freely tradable. As long as you have a willing seller and a willing buyer and a price that is right, we should do the deal! Emotion should not stop the business sense of the deal.

SO WHAT IS NEXT FOR RHL?

The rationale for the sale is therefore clear. Raffles stands to gain S$605 million and will distribute 40 cents per share to

lers. The balance of the proceeds from the sale will
ilance sheet and with a conservative gearing, the
l have a good financial war chest at its disposal
_ _..._ on other, possibly more profitable, businesses!

A special board committee will be appointed to study the forward strategy for RHL, but I can tell you that we are not short of opportunities.

WHAT IS MY PERSONAL SENTIMENT?

On a personal note, after five years of association with Raffles Hotel group, I am also very much emotionally attached to it. I have always stayed in a Raffles or Swissotel hotel whenever I travelled abroad, both for leisure or business. In Singapore, except for the China Club[3], I always patronise our restaurants in our Raffles Hotel group. And I use the Amrita Spa almost every morning for my workout. It is the best start to my day. The facilities and services are first class, and on some rare occasions where there has been a lapse of services, I will unfailingly notify them and they do react fast. I have also in my career personally built or helped build many buildings to which I have developed some emotional attachment, including Changi Airport, Suzhou Sheraton Hotel, Four Seasons in Canary Wharf, Capital Tower, The Loft and many more. I have to remain steadfast, not to get emotional about them and must view them as my achievements and take pride in the fact that I have created something well and then move on.

I have often consoled myself by saying, "We don't have to own it to love it!"

End Notes

1 In July 2005, Raffles Holdings, controlled by CapitaLand, sold all its 41 hotels and resorts, including the renowned Raffles Hotel in Singapore, to US-based investment fund Colony Capital LLC for S$1.72 billion (US$1 billion), including debt.

2 Severe acute respiratory syndrome or SARS is a respiratory disease in humans which is caused by the SARS corona virus. There has been one major epidemic to date, between November 2002 and July 2003, with 8,096 known cases of the disease, and 774 deaths (a mortality rate of 9.6%) being listed in the World Health Organisation's April 21, 2004 concluding report.

3 The China Club Singapore, located on 52nd floor of Capital Tower, is an exclusive and private dining club. The club is designed by the founder of China Club, David Tang, who is also famed for his Shanghai Tang boutiques.

Liew Mun Leong/President & CEO **11/05/2006** 06:19 PM

To: All Staff

cc: Board of Directors

bcc:

Subject: **Cutting Red Tape**

Cap/taLand

... Building People

A s our businesses expand rapidly and the number of our markets grows, there is sometimes a natural tendency for the layers in the organisation to also grow to deal with the increasing complexity of our business/corporate structure. The problem with this is that organisational layers can breed bureaucracy and slow down the company. We recognised this potential problem some years back (prior to the merger between Pidemco Land and DBS Land), and as a practical solution, I took the decision to keep the organisation as flat as we could. I believe that this should still be the case today.

A recent memo (not a board paper) came to me after going through four other signatories. This is crazy! Clearing with one person is good enough and others can be copied on it. We don't need so many levels of authority to agree on a memo before it comes to me.

We pride ourselves in being fast and decisive in our business decisions and we have won many partners and deals because of our fast response. We are a commercial company. We have to act quickly. We do not want to give the impression, whether to our staff or to outsiders, that ours is a bureaucratic organisation. Please do look out for red tape so that it does not take root and grow in our organisation. If you come across it, tell us about it and we will make changes.

Let me take you through another matter regarding efficiency in communication. Quite often when I ask someone to look into something, I fail to get any feedback until I enquire about what has happened to the matter. The task may or may not have been successfully accomplished, but I should not be kept in the dark and have to ask for the latest update. This is not another bureaucratic process of reporting, as I am only interested in keeping up on what's happening.

I have said before—I don't need to approve everything, but I do like to stay on top of what matters. A short email, SMS or telephone call will do. And please do that not only with me, but also with others who need to be kept informed. It will keep us all connected!

Liew Mun Leong/President & CEO **01/11/2006** 05:22 PM

To: All Staff

cc: Board of Directors

bcc:

Subject: **Turn Off those Annoying Toys!**

Cap/taLand

Building People

I recently discovered that the wonderful technology of handphones and the Blackberry can unwittingly become a serious addiction amongst us. They are unconsciously, but obnoxiously, overused or misused whilst we are attending meetings or ostensibly engaged in a conversation. This increasingly common delinquency, especially amongst our senior colleagues who should know better, may be quite annoying and indeed unforgivable as it depicts a "couldn't-care-less" attitude and a lack of respect for others.

No doubt, the handphone is easily one of the greatest communication tools of the last 10 years. We can now easily reach any part of the civilised world at any time. And so is the Blackberry, which is now my "must-have" handheld office computer. Wherever I have to travel, it now serves as an effective, all-powerful "time killer" and "time saver" at any airport or any other place where I have to wait. I can whip out my Blackberry and clear most if not all of my incoming emails whilst standing in the agonisingly long immigration line. For example, I crafted this email on my Blackberry whilst flying back from Moscow and stored it in the save box to be sent later.

On the other hand, many users, including some of our senior colleagues, have grown too addicted to these two little powerful yet demanding electronic devices. They now can't live without reaching for them 24/7. Frequently, they are seen using their handphone and/or Blackberry during meetings (or worse, even during serious negotiations), reading or sending SMSes or emails, blatantly and disrespectfully ignoring the ongoing discussion. Some are even as rude as to conduct a separate telephone conversation whilst sitting at a live meeting. Speaking in a very soft whisper on the phone will still disrupt the meeting.

We should know that such behaviour at an ongoing meeting:

(a) is very rude and is completely disrespectful;
(b) is anti-social; and
(c) is very distracting and disrupts the ongoing discussion.

If you are not interested in the discussion, then leave the meeting. It is unproductive to stay on if you have no interest there!

Procedurally, before the meeting, put your devices on silent mode or switch them off.

Unless you need to be contacted urgently, like waiting to close a billion dollar deal, you should wait until the meeting has ended to go back to your SMS or Blackberry's email. Most of the time, the message can wait. If a call does come in that you have to respond to, I suggest you quietly leave the meeting to answer it.

You certainly can't impress anyone if you hug your handphone or Blackberry and appear very busy with it right in the midst of an important meeting. I, for one, wouldn't be very impressed with your demonstration of multi-tasking skills.

I suspect, and understand, that such an addiction to your handphone and Blackberry may be reflective of your commitment to be connected to your office messages constantly. But we must also appreciate that it is rude to do so.

Sometimes, I am guilty of this misbehaviour, but it is usually because I am getting bored with the discussion or I am feeling sleepy and want to do something to keep myself awake. These are not valid excuses and I will not repeat it again.

I hope you are not reading this rather lengthy email whilst attending a meeting. If so, turn it off right now!! And keep those annoying toys away at meetings.

Chapter 4

Learning Journeys

"Shareholders invest money in the company, not emotions. They want financial returns not emotional returns."

I can spend as much as a third of the year on the road, and in some years, more. From China to Los Angeles, such trips can often be demanding. Yet they are great opportunities to draw lessons from different cultures and social and business environments, to understand not only our competitors and partners better, but also our clients and their needs.

I like to relate my travel observations in my emails to share what my eyes have been opened to. Take, for example, global competition.

The Chinese in particular offer great insights into competition, and pose a very serious global threat to everyone. If you think about it, what is it that you can do that they cannot do? I recall that they can produce a good quality pen at way below S$1 (US$0.67)—they are selling it at that price! That's something we will never be able to do. If they can produce things so cheaply, how can we compete on anything against them? Being creative is what will help us to survive.

If you can compete against the Chinese successfully, then you can compete against anybody else. You will certainly have a place to live in the world. But you've got to open your eyes to how fast they are advancing to compete with the world. Be there, be anywhere, and learn!

Liew Mun Leong/President & CEO **14/09/1998** 07:37 AM

To: All Staff

cc: Board of Directors

bcc:

Subject: **Opportunities in Lean Times**

Cap/taLand

... Building People

L ast week, I made a short trip to Hanoi to prepare for the official opening of the Meritus Westlake Hotel.

Hanoi currently looks very much like the Singapore I knew in the early 1950s when I was a young boy. It is outmoded in its architectural design, but it is quite clean. The streets' business activities show remarkable entrepreneurship with vendors displaying all kinds of goods that may have the smallest economic values; offer it for sale and someone will buy it.

The people work very hard in that country. Notwithstanding the hardship and meagre average salary of less than US$100 per month, many of them spend their spare time going for classes to improve themselves—English language, book-keeping, anything that will prepare them better in their new free-market economy.

One typical characteristic that always puzzles me is that in Hanoi, you will never find a plump or obese person among the four million living in the whole city. The Vietnamese are very slender and thin. We speculate that it is either the diet or the hard work they have put themselves to. And this brings me to a very enterprising idea I saw in the city.

I saw a woman sitting on the street, next to a weighing scale. I was curious and asked our local accountant Tam Kam Jiunn[1] what she was selling. Tam told me that she sells the service of a weighing scale to the local people who want to weigh themselves. She charges 500 dongs, which is approximately S$0.04 (US$0.02), to weigh each person. I did not understand this business prospect because everybody is so thin. In Singapore, everyone who weighs himself wants to know how much weight he's lost! I asked, "What is the motivation to weigh themselves?" Tam told me that the Vietnamese, being thin, like to become fat to look prosperous. However, they want to keep track of how fat they are growing and this lady has identified that as an opportunity!

This story is amusing to me, but it underlines the high degree of entrepreneurship that can be exhibited even in hard times. Find the need and there will be buyers even in difficult times.

We also visited several famous Vietnamese artists' homes to review their artwork, which we were buying for the hotel we were building in Hanoi. We walked through dark alleys and broken corners to reach their residences. Vietnamese painters are an interesting lot. Despite the long years of the Vietnam War, their paintings are not dull or oppressive, but brilliant colours are used. Their link with French artists probably still influences them. The paintings are outstanding and well-priced compared to our Singaporean artists. They seem to understand supply and demand well and do not enter into loose or frivolous negotiations. They know their value!

Lessons to learn:

1. Even in poor times, one can still find opportunities to make a living.

2. Younger Singaporeans should visit a city like Hanoi (or Yangon in Myanmar) to see how hard people work to make a living. They still persevere. Young Singaporeans don't appreciate what Singapore was like in the 1950s and this can be a good playback in time to show how far we have come.

End Note

1 Tam Kam Jiunn is now a Tax Executive with CapitaLand Limited.

Liew Mun Leong/President & CEO **30/05/1999** 08:33 PM

To: All Staff

cc: Board of Directors

bcc:

Subject: **Bluewater Vision**

Cap/taLand

... Building People

With a built-up area of 1.6 million sq ft (148,640 sq m), Bluewater, located south-east of London, is arguably the largest shopping mall in Europe. Just opened in March, this mega mall has, against all odds and imagination, been highly successful and a rewarding investment for the owner.

Whilst they expected 80,000 visitors a day, more than 100,000 shoppers from all over the UK and Europe have been happily pouring in every day since the opening. Each shopper has been spending an average of £29 (US$46.98) against the forecast of £22. Envious retailers in London, particularly those on Oxford Street and Bond Street, have been protesting about how such suburban malls are hurting their business. They claim that it will threaten the city's economy. Many think that the government will not approve any other similar suburban malls again!

So what is the secret to this daring but successful and profitable project?

The site was an old chalk quarry, abandoned after decades of quarrying by the land's owner, Bluecircle, a large cement manufacturer. Over time, it became filled with rainwater and had become a huge manmade, abandoned lake (3 kilometres by 1.5 kilometres). Bluecircle and a few developers, including a reputable British contractor, formed a consortium to develop the area but somehow failed. Australian developer Lend Lease entered the scene. The company had been looking around the UK for opportunities and they came up with the bold development vision for this site.

They did plenty of research and ground studies. They found that about 11 million people live within an hour's drive and these people could possibly spend £5.6 billion a year on shopping there if a good mall was available. Painstakingly, they interviewed 35,000 people to find out about their needs and wish lists, from tenant mix to security and parking lots. They provided 13,000 free car parking spaces that are 25% wider than the standard.

There are concierge points at the five lobbies to meet personal needs, including lockers, resting sofas and the largest children's crèche in Europe (parents are given pagers in case their kids need them).

There are family toilets for diaper changes, and they are well-equipped with warmers and microwaves. For security, they have collaborated with the local "bobbies" (local police officers) to help patrol the area, including the car parks. Apparently an average of 24 cars are stolen every week in the neighbouring shopping mall. So far, with the local Bobbies involved, it's not been an issue at this new mega shopping mall.

There are different shopping destinations within the mall for children, women and men, and plenty of F&B outlets (on average, shoppers eat twice per trip) and lots of sofas to rest tired legs—somehow these are never found in Singapore. As for tenant mix, they have everybody there, with many international retailers making their first forays in the UK!

So what have we learnt from this inspirational turnaround project?

(1) Lend Lease is very successful in building retail malls in Australia. If you are competent, you can export your expertise globally, even far away and against the best in advanced countries. But would you dare to take the risk?

(2) To be world class, we've got to have a vision and a bold vision, too. Lend Lease was very visionary and bold to think and act on this opportunity far away from its home base. But it was cautious and did plenty of careful research. It had the expertise in building retail malls (and also civil engineering skills), and with hard-nosed thinking and arduous work, it succeeded.

(3) Understanding customers and meeting their needs are very important. In Bluewater, it went out of its way to please customers. Every little detail counts.

(4) When we were walking around, a group from Taiwan told the project architect they were so impressed with what they'd seen that they wanted to discuss how they could work together to start one in Taiwan. When you do something so successful, it will bring reputation and more success. Others will approach you, as has been demonstrated by the many countries that have approached Singapore to help build a Changi Airport for them!

(5) To me, the most important lesson is that we've got to have a bold vision—to turn a big, abandoned water hole into one huge world-class shopping mall. There are civil

engineering challenges and business judgements to take. And then there must be the courage and perseverance to do it.

Can we do it?

Liew Mun Leong/President & CEO **02/10/1999** 05:13 PM
    To: All Staff
    cc: Board of Directors
    bcc:
Subject: **Vegetable Washing Machines**

Cap/taLand

... Building People

S ome anecdotes from the Fortune Global Forum, which I attended last week in Shanghai:

When Zhang Ruimin[1] took over Haier Group some seven or eight years ago, it was in a big mess. This Chinese company, which produced washing machines and refrigerators in Shanghai, was on the brink of bankruptcy. Its products did not sell well even domestically, let alone internationally, because of poor quality. Morale was down as workers were retrenched. What could he do as the new man in charge?

Lesson No. 1 – He used an interesting way to change the workers' attitudes towards quality. He lined up all the poor-quality washing machines and fridges and labelled them with the names of workers and supervisors who were responsible for these unsold products that were lying wastefully in the warehouse. Workers were then given sledgehammers and were instructed to smash them all one by one. He began it himself, to show that he had overall responsibility for the whole factory. The "destruction show" was dramatic and emotionally shocked the workers as each machine would have cost as much as their whole year's salary. The quality lessons sunk deep into the workers and now the company is producing machines with high-quality standards that enable it to be marketed internationally.

Lesson No. 2 – When the company first tried to sell to Iran, nobody knew its products and the first 10,000 units that had been exported there were not selling well. The local agent advised Haier to lower prices drastically to compete. Zhang Ruimin refused as he felt the quality was as good as any Western model. Eventually, some were sold and the products' reputation won over the market in Iran. Consumers found Haier to be just as good as other brands and the products were relatively cheaper. If the quality is good, customers will pay for it!

Lesson No. 3 – Recently Zhang Ruimin received unusually high reports of breakdowns among the company's washing machines sold in Sichuan. Yet, they were good-quality machines, so what was happening? Field studies showed that customers there decided to use the washing machines not only to wash clothes but also to wash produce from their farms, like sweet potatoes and vegetables. What did he do? He ordered his engineers to design a new washing machine that could indeed also wash vegetables and sweet potatoes. It sounds funny, but if that is what the customers there want, let's get them one! They now sell dual purpose washing machines in Sichuan and they sell well! Innovation and entrepreneurship at its best.

Today, Haier Group is one of the most successful manufacturing companies in China, with more than US$1 billion worth of sales and commanding a good share of both the domestic and international markets with a fine reputation for quality. What a major transformation and a sharp contrast with the same company that a few years back was rundown, almost insolvent and had an image of making poor-quality products.

Quality, innovation and entrepreneurship can do much for us—if we try!

I don't expect to have to use a sledgehammer to smash a condominium building in order to teach our people about quality. But these lessons of improving quality, innovation and entrepreneurship should be learnt, although maybe in a less destructive way.

End Note

1 Zhang Ruimin – CEO of Haier Group Company; he is the first chinese business leader to have lectured at Harvard. Haier Group was adopted as case study material for Harvard Business School, which was the first among chinese companies.

Liew Mun Leong/President & CEO **08/12/1999** 07:13 PM

To: All Staff

cc: Board of Directors

bcc:

Subject: **Meeting with a Shanghai Mayor**

CapitaLand

... Building People

C hairman Philip Yeo[1] recently asked me to meet Han Zheng,[2] vice mayor of Shanghai, to explore housing projects. Vice Mayor Han (a vice minister in status) is in charge of development, infrastructure and construction in the city.

I met him on a Monday morning and he told me a surprising but pleasant introductory story.

Prior to our meeting he had visited incognito our Shanghai Regency serviced apartment on a Saturday night, posing as a real estate businessman interested in looking around our facilities. Our guest relationship manager, Rafidah, spoke fluent Mandarin and received him well. He was surprised that although he introduced himself as a possible competitor, Rafidah was hospitable and energetically showed him around. He was impressed with our design and construction of our development—he said the rooms were sophisticated in layout and yet not ostentatious, unlike, he pointed out, some hotels in Shanghai. He also praised our maintenance standards, adding that there was no point building expensive buildings and not maintaining them well. He complimented us for having polite staff who courteously greeted him during his tour of the property. He pointed out to his officials that ours was an exemplary investment in Shanghai. It was not only optimally built, but well-managed and we trained our staff well.

The purpose of his visit was, I guessed, to check us out. He was obviously pleased with our investment both in real estate and in how we trained "the local people". I told him that we concentrated on both "hardware" and "software".

I am impressed with this relatively young vice mayor, who is probably in his late 40s.

He had taken the trouble to spend a Saturday evening to find out the background of the investor he was about to meet to prepare himself for a more meaningful discussion. It shows that he cares.

Not long ago, Chinese officials were quite bureaucratic and expected a high degree of respect before we could even start talking business with them. Now things have changed. They do their homework before they even meet us!

Two lessons here:

(i) We should always give the best reception and services to our customers—whoever walks in to talk to us. Rafidah had put on a good show and she won the day for us. She could have ignored Vice Mayor Han since he posed as a competitor.

(ii) We must always do our homework on the people that we are meeting—check them out and be interested in them.

In China, even high-ranking officials are making this effort.

Can we, in our serviced apartments, retail malls and office complexes, consistently give good quality service to whoever comes to see us? The right attitude and consistent service quality must be maintained—even during surprise checks.

Vice Mayor Han is serious about the relationship with his investors. He rightly treats them as customers. He wants to create a strong impact on his customers and he bothers to make the extra effort, even on a Saturday evening, to check out the background of the investors. How do we spend our Saturday nights?

End Notes

1 Philip Yeo was chairman of Pidemco Land, and the founding chairman of CapitaLand until 2003. He is now the chairman of CapitaLand's International Advisory Board.
2 Han Zheng was appointed the mayor of Shanghai in February 2003.

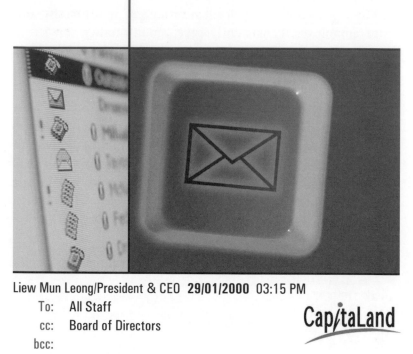

Liew Mun Leong/President & CEO **29/01/2000** 03:15 PM

To: All Staff

cc: Board of Directors

bcc:

Subject: **Speak Up, Man!**

Cap/taLand

... Building People

A fortnight ago, I attended a CEO forum in the very old medieval city of Bruges near Brussels. Plenty to learn, yet I came to understand why a past participant (Boon Swan Foo,[1] CEO of ST Engineering[2]) described the annual forum as a very "humiliating experience".

There were 30 participants, all CEOs or their No. 2 from very large, world-class companies—global multinationals, much larger than us, e.g. IBM, British Steel, Cable and Wireless, 3M, Unilever, Deutsche Bank, Hyundai, Tokyo Electric Power, BBC.

Don't muck around with them, I said to myself. They are all "Top Dogs" and "Big Hitters". The majority of participants were Europeans and Americans, but there was also one Dominican, three Japanese, one Korean and one other Singaporean. I made a deliberate attempt to study and observe them carefully—their behaviour, performances and characteristics.

As expected, they were all bright, clever and experienced corporate climbers and full of energy (at whatever age they may be; ranging from early 40s to 60s).

We discussed issues at open forums as well as in teams of six to 10. One clear commonality is that they were all very vocal and spoke their minds. In fact, some were so domineering that some of us had to interrupt them to get a chance to speak. The point is, the more reticent you are, the more you can be left out in the cold.

But it is not their style and behaviour that is important—it is their analytical skills, clarity of thought and their ability to speak their mind that alerted me to the differences between them and us.

Why can't our people back home do that? We do have very clever people, but they are not in the habit of speaking their minds!

For some time, I have been prompting our colleagues not only to open their mouths, but also to speak their minds. We preach about honesty and integrity all the time. But intellectual integrity is just as important for us as it may be costly if we do not offer straight, honest opinions to our bosses!

"Yes men" are not healthy for our organisation. They are, in fact, dangerous, as a wrong judgement may have been made. If you think the boss is wrong, tell him (or her) and have a healthy debate about it. Good bosses will appreciate you more and begin to value your views. Remember the story of "The Emperor's New Clothes"?

On the other hand, don't start by saying "NO, NO, NO" to new ideas or being defensive when faced with some criticism.

So, speak up, be honest and be bold enough to say what you wish to say. In Pidemco Land, I assure you that you will not be penalised for speaking up, as we value opinion from everyone in the company.

End Notes

1 Boon Swan Foo is now managing director of A*STAR, (Agency of Science, Technology & Research) & executive chairman of Exploit Technologies.
2 ST Engineering was a sister company of Pidemco Land; both were subsidiaries of Singapore Technologies Pte Ltd.

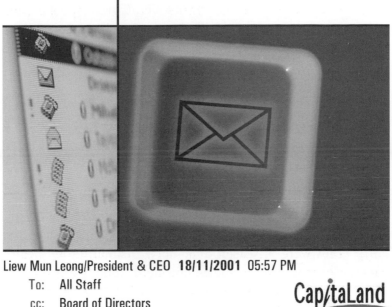

Liew Mun Leong/President & CEO **18/11/2001** 05:57 PM

To: All Staff

cc: Board of Directors

bcc:

Subject: **Price-gap Opportunities**

Cap/taLand

... Building People

S hanghai is now an unbelievably booming city. Every corner of the city is visibly bursting with energy. Shopping malls and restaurants, both for locals and foreigners, in fact, all places for any human activity, are full. People look happy and are smiling all the time. At a traffic stop, I sighted a very ordinary looking newspaper vendor couple—the wife was busy distributing newspapers and the husband was helping out in their simple business transactions. He was smiling, singing and literally dancing around his wife while carrying out his duty of collecting money. Not a really sophisticated business with big returns, I guessed, but they were simply happy with themselves.

111

Let me relate some contrasting experiences in this marketplace where I see opportunities for us.

The latest in-thing restaurant complex in Shanghai is called "Xintiandi" (新天地)—a collection of very stylishly designed restaurants housed within several rows of rehabilitated buildings. These eateries are always packed and a reservation is always necessary. Here, you can witness the strong spending power of the Shanghainese. Yet there is a great price gap or price/value factor that I cannot understand.

For example, three of us drank coffee at a rather casual coffee joint and the bill came to RMB80 (US$9.70). One RMB has about the same spending power as S$1 and if you were earning RMB you would feel the pinch. It is difficult to analyse how the local consumers can earn enough to spend this way.

Let me tell you about other "pricing anomalies".

We went to a simple Chinese restaurant called "Gap", patronised by locals and some foreigners. The famous Shanghai hairy crabs were in season and, notwithstanding my health concern over unhealthy high-cholesterol food, I ordered one crab for each of my guests. They proved to be delicious, but cost RMB280 each! Although it hurt my pocket, I thought if the Shanghainese could afford them on whatever they were earning, I should not chicken out. I quietly paid the costly bill from my own pocket, but secretly groaned over what I could have bought with that money.

Another day, we went to a market at "Yu Yuan" (豫园), which was jam-packed with thousands of locals and tourists. There I discovered the opposite pricing shocks. Several roadside stores were selling gold-framed reading glasses that could be neatly folded into nicely designed velvet pocket boxes. The quality appeared very good and they even catered for varying degrees of long-sightedness. Guess how much they were going for? RMB10 each! How could they produce them at such ridiculously low prices? Cheap labour, low production costs! How do we compete with them?

Walking further down the road, I saw a 10-year-old girl dragging her younger brother to a stall selling steaming-hot sweet potatoes—a reminiscence of my poor but happy younger days. We don't sell such treats now in Singapore, I lamented. She cheerfully told the hawker that she wanted to buy a RMB0.50 sweet potato. The hawker was equally enthusiastic with his young customers' order and handed her a king-sized sweet potato. That large sweet potato could feed the two young kids for lunch! Again, further down the road they were selling deep-fried chive cakes at four for RMB1! How could food be so much cheaper compared to the hairy crab the night before?

So, there you are. You have to pay RMB280 for a hairy crab at one extreme, and a king-sized sweet potato for RMB0.50 or a pair of well-designed reading glasses for RMB10 at the other extreme. We are now marketing a new project called Manhattan Heights selling at around RMB1.2 million (about S$250,000) for a three-room apartment. It is selling very well and several Shanghainese bought these new homes with hard RMB cash brought to the showrooms—in other words, no borrowing!

In developing countries, there is always this phenomenon— some things are very cheap and in sharp contrast to some other things that are very expensive. So those who can afford will buy the lavishly-priced things and those who can't will have to settle with the normal-priced goods or services.

How big is the market for both extremes? In Shanghai, this pricing/value gap is huge. Between the high selling price and the actual low cost, there are opportunities to make money—that's for our entrepreneurs to think about. Capture the low cost and identify the high-price market, products or opportunities and you will be making your fortunes there. Go for it, guys!

Liew Mun Leong/President & CEO **01/07/2002** 04:46 PM

To: All Staff

cc: Board of Directors

bcc:

Subject: **Confronting Competitive China**

Cap/taLand

... Building People

E very time I visit China, I get really frightened with the competitiveness that I encounter there. My latest trip was no exception.

I have seen several Chinese vendors selling exact replicas of Montblanc pens, in various designs and with identical details and finishes. It feels and writes as well as any other Montblanc pen. No smearing or blockages.

Last year, these pens sold for more than RMB100 each, then prices dropped to RMB70 (1 RMB = US12 cents). At the beginning of this year, they were sold at RMB40. Two months ago, they were going for only RMB15 (US$1.82). Putting aside the brand imitation value, they are as good as any other writing instrument.

In my latest trip, guess how much the pens are going for? Only RMB7! Looking at the pen, it's difficult to understand how they can produce pens with such finishes and still sell it at less than S$1.60 (US$0.91). This includes distribution and retail profit, which means the manufacturer's cost will be not more than RMB4 or RMB5. A normal, disposable ballpoint pen in Singapore would have cost that much or more. Even the metal and its gold or silver plating would have cost more anywhere else. The cost structure is frighteningly cheap. For S$1.15, one can use, lose and throw them away like any other disposable pen; except that they look much too good.

The young vendor who was selling these pens looked really hungry. He was friendly, persistent and very interested in his customers—not the "take it or leave it attitude" we sometimes meet in Singapore!

I am not supporting imitation or fake products, but the moral of the story is, can we compete with these guys now? Do we appreciate the seriousness of the competition out there in China?

What is there that we can do that they can't? I asked one of the journalists who interviewed me about her views of Shanghai. The first thing she told me was that she wanted to start a trading business there—buy cheap from within China and export into Singapore or elsewhere!

Interestingly, in the '70s, several Westerners who came to Singapore told me the same entrepreneurial thinking—start an import/export company here, buy cheap and send to Europe/ America! It is just China's turn now.

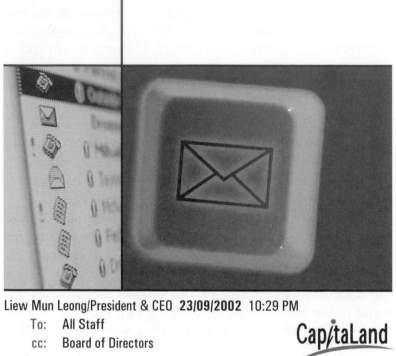

Liew Mun Leong/President & CEO **23/09/2002** 10:29 PM

To: All Staff

cc: Board of Directors

bcc:

Subject: **Survival Creativity**

Cap/taLand

... Building People

Recently, I asked Minister Lim Boon Heng[1] how bad our unemployment situation was. He replied that it was easing off slightly, but he was concerned with the attitude of some Singaporeans who were being very choosy about job opportunities—complaining a job is too far away or that they will have to miss their favourite TV shows, etc. I told him this story:

Xi'an, the once glorious capital of ancient China, is now a very poor city. It has no visible economy except tourism, which it only recently started capitalising on following the accidental discovery of the terracotta army of the first emperor of China. Ancient tombs of past emperors or empresses are their "factory" to bring in money to the city. As in other central cities in China, joblessness is commonplace. Jobless men are often seen plying the streets with the tools of their humble trades, offering to do any chores, anywhere for a few RMB.

Whilst visiting Xi'an one evening, I went to a toilet in a restaurant and experienced a strange service that I am sure you have not heard of. I was standing up easing myself (sorry for being graphic here) when suddenly I felt a pair of hands on my shoulders and before I knew it, I was given a gentle massage. I turned around and saw this young, tallish boy trying his amateurish massage on my shoulders and back and asking me whether I needed gentler or stronger pressure. It was quite shocking and very embarrassing given the situation. But I thought it would be very rude or unkind to him if I stopped him completely. Whilst washing my hands subsequently, he turned off the tap, offered a towel and comb and bade me thank you and good night with a bow. A few RMB notes flew out of my pocket.

A colleague went to the same toilet later and got the same, unsolicited treatment. But he admitted he was too embarrassed to let the boy carry on with such service and stopped him. Guess what the Chinese boy did? He brought a towel and started to clean his shoes instead! Again, a few RMB notes came out of my colleague's pocket.

Is it humiliating to earn a few RMB this way? Some Singaporeans may think so. But if you are poor and hungry, this seems a really innovative way to earn a living. Pushed to a corner, we would have to do something to survive. Could we be more creative? Still thinking about your job being more than one hour away from home or missing your favourite TV stars? Think again about what others have to do to make a living. Think we live in a different world? Two thousand years ago, what was Singapore, compared to the all-powerful capital city of ancient China—Xi'an?

I went home shuddering with the thought of what my children, grandchildren or great grandchildren may have to do one day to earn a living!

End Note

1 Lim Boon Heng, the minister in the prime minister's office and a member of the cabinet of Singapore, was at the time of writing the secretary-general of the National Trades Union Congress.

Liew Mun Leong/President & CEO **16/12/2002** 06:24 PM

To: All Staff

cc: Board of Directors

bcc:

Subject: **Every Business Needs a China Strategy**

Cap/taLand

... Building People

A lawyer who recently travelled a fair bit to China made an interesting observation. When drafting initial public offering (IPO) prospectuses in Singapore before year 2000, it was the practice to include a statement on how a listing company would address two topical issues that could affect its future:

(a) The Y2K problem (I think this was an SGX requirement).

(b) The company's Internet strategy (this was, I think, not an SGX requirement, but a competitive strategy to disclose.)

This lawyer now believes it wouldn't be a surprise if IPO aspirants are expected to craft out a separate statement on the company's "China strategy"!

China's economic growth is now dramatically affecting the whole global economy. How do we take on 1.3 billion people with an explosive economy still growing faster than most modern economies? It has a huge domestic sector, with frighteningly low manufacturing costs and a fast catching-up technology base. Each time I visit China—and I have been travelling there for 20 years—I sense a stronger and stronger influence by China on our business, indeed, on every possible business! It is a real force to be reckoned with, my friends!

For survival, every company, whether domestic or global, must think through its China strategy before it is too late. Even if you are running a small business, anything you produce or sell, China will do it faster, much cheaper and with comparable, if not better, quality. Even if you can do it better now, China will catch up quickly.

China is certainly more crucial to address than Y2K or the Internet threat, both of which we can spend money to resolve.

Liew Mun Leong/President & CEO **23/12/2002** 06:22 PM

To: All Staff

cc: Board of Directors

bcc:

Subject: **Black Belt vs. Black Belt**

Cap/taLand

... Building People

H an Fook Kwang, managing editor at the Straits Times,[1] once asked me what, as a developer, we can do that the Chinese developers in Shanghai can't. How long would they take to catch up with us? I proudly suggested quality, reliability, CapitaLand's international experience and reputation, etc, and feebly guessed that within three to five years, they would catch up with us. On second thought, it will probably be faster than that. Let's see.

Five years ago, they needed our capital investment. Now they don't need our money and very soon—I am sure within my career—we (including the West) will need their money! A reverse investment flow from China to Singapore and the West will happen. I will bet on that.

Five years ago, they produced poor-quality homes. Our driver in Suzhou happily bought his own apartment. It was a bare, raw concrete "core and shell" with unpainted walls; water points without any taps, basins or sanitary fittings; and electrical wires that were unconnected. Only commonly used toilets and bathrooms were provided—much like Singapore's first generation of public housing in the '60s. But for him, it was already a huge step forward.

Now in Shanghai they are building full-scale, modern-design condominiums with fully finished kitchens, cupboards, air-conditioning, club houses and lustrous landscaping. We may have introduced these development concepts, but the Chinese have followed quickly and with even greater zeal. Economy of scale spreads the high fee costs and they willingly engage top American architects and interior and landscape designers. We took 35 years to reach where we are now. They did it in five! No, they won't need three to five years to reach our product standards!

Five years ago, there were hardly any professional managers working for them. Now they are filled with professional engineers, architects and MBA'ers. Many are trained at the best Western universities. I met several of them and they were just as capable as ours, or those from any other country. In some cases, they are even better. One observation—their managers are much more entrepreneurial than ours. They are younger, hungrier and want to catch up on lost time. These, to me, are their biggest challenging factors to us—people, managers and leaders!

We can no longer compete with them on the basis of their weakness. They don't need our money, or to borrow our design or quality programmes, and their human resources are competitive and abundant. There is nothing that we can do that they can't. We just have to match them strength for strength. That is a given in globalisation—all competitive factors get levelled out fast, and we have just got to be better and ahead of the competition. It is a "black belt vs. another black belt". The next generation of "black belts" will have a very tough battle to fight, not only in China, but everywhere in this competitive, global market.

It happened to Japan. It dominated in the '70s and '80s with its strong economy. Singapore received its investments and technology and we learnt to become better. There is some reverse investment traffic now.

Merry X'mas and a Happy New Year—But think about it, Mr or Ms Black Belt!

End Note

1 *The Straits Times* is one of Singapore's daily newspapers.

Liew Mun Leong/President & CEO **16/03/2004** 06:04 PM
  To: All Staff
  cc: Board of Directors
  bcc:
Subject: **Takeaways from India**

CapitaLand

... Building People

S everal colleagues at the CapitaLand Management Programme prompted me to continue my weekend emails. Sorry I have slackened because the last few months have been extremely hectic for me, what with the year-end results, overseas roadshows, etc.

Here are some "takeaways" from a recent trip to India involving several of our CEOs:

(1) Except for Anthony Seah and myself, none of our CEOs had ever been to India, let alone worked there. So, if we were to do business in India, the big question was, "Who would

be the co-ordinating CEO?" We were touring a business park when Kee Teck Koon asked Jennie Chua,[1] who was marching in front of the group, whether she was "fighting" for the big job. The reply was a big "No" and she quickly retreated. This reminded me of my first lesson from my army days: never volunteer for anything!

Our Indian host said to us, "My mother told me never to stand behind a horse or in front of the boss!" This is a wise Indian saying indeed.

(2) We met several Indian business groups. They made excellent presentations and were very articulate. They had done their homework and researched on us and our business interests. They were all great communicators. Here are some great nuggets:

(a) When asked how we could contribute to them as a partner or why they chose us, one said, "Brand, brand, brand. Ten reasons and reasons numbers one to nine are brand, brand and brand."

(b) On India's bureaucracy, one proudly told us that there are no more long delays. He can get his building plans approved within one day! We must give feedback to our URA[2] and BCA[3] on this!

(c) Foreigners are not allowed to invest in real estate in India unless it is a minimum 100-acre (404685.64 sq m) township development. One Indian developer told us about his profitable township project. "Our land values appreciated four times within six months. In my township project we are turning soil into gold!" Another gold rush in the making?[4]

(d) India has not obviously progressed well in town urbanisation. The many fundamental reasons include outdated real estate laws and regulations based, ironically, on socialism for the protection of the poor, human rights, etc. Mumbai's slums are sorrowful scenes of abject poverty—an almost surreal sight for some seeing it for the first time. The dilapidated buildings even in the central business district appeared abandoned; Jennie Chua asked innocently whether they were occupied, but of course they are. Mumbai still has some of the most expensive office space in the world! My host didn't quite believe me when I told him that Singapore's buildings have to be painted every five years. I quietly reflected on the tremendous effort it would need to transform the slums in Mumbai to a decent, modern city standard. I told myself: "It will require no less than the hand of God!"

(e) My sense—and this was quite apparent to us during our visit—is that there is one fundamental, but powerful, reason why the slums and "un-development" is still going on. One key word summarises it: Protectionism. Foreigners are discouraged from investing in real estate in India. They cited the bad example of how Bangkok and Seoul had suffered adversely when foreigners speculated on real estate there.

Now, several quarters acknowledge protectionism by the local developers. Some cry out for reforms, but politics gets into the way of good intentions.

No wonder that Arun Shourie, who is India's Minister of Disinvestment, Communication and Information Technology, drew the differences between India and China: "In India, everybody has a veto". But he is not giving up. "Governance is not golf. That we are a democracy does not entitle us to a handicap." Bravo, Mr Shourie!

Our host joked that elsewhere around the world, the fastest way to make big money is either through drugs or gun-running. "Here, it is real estate!" A bad joke, but a reality?

Whilst touring Mumbai I told Jennie Chua that if any guy still brands Singapore as "boring" (which many I know do), send him to Mumbai to take a look at what life here is all about. When you see children sleeping openly in grass ditches or using sewage pipes as their homes, you will not find Singapore so boring after all. HDB is heaven on earth!

I am now even more convinced about our company tag line, "Building for people to build people"!

End Notes

1 Jennie Chua was then president and CEO of Raffles Holdings. She is now President and CEO of the Ascott Group.
2 URA is Urban Redevelopment Authority in Singapore.
3 BCA is the Building and Construction Authority in Singapore.
4 India subsequently eased its rules on inward investment in the construction industry in early 2005, cutting the size requirement for townships built with foreign investment to 25 acres, with the minimum size for a commercial project set at 538,195 sq ft (50,000 sq m).

Liew Mun Leong/President & CEO **21/08/2006** 10:06 PM

To: All Staff

cc: Board of Directors

bcc:

Cap/taLand

Subject: **Learning from a Chengdu Developer**

... Building People

Y ou have probably read that farmers in China often clash with developers over acquisition of their farm land for property development. Does it have to be so acrimonious all the time? Not necessarily. Let me tell you about one developer to whom the farmers love to hand over their land willingly.

Recently we started a 50:50 joint venture company with a local Chengdu developer called Zhixin to build affordable housing projects in Chengdu. One of the reasons why we selected it as a partner is because this is a rare group that the local farmers seem to love. Let me tell you how the chairman of Zhixin, Yang Hao, wins them over.

Yang Hao showed us one impressive project Zhixin built for local farmers as part of the acquisition settlement. It is called New Britain Town, designed with details such as red brickwork and ornamental iron gates.

The key to his success is not just the appealing, westernised design detailing alone, but the specially packaged compensation offer itself. By government requirements, the developer has to build compensatory family housing for the farmer equivalent to 30 sq m (323 sq ft) per head. In this project they generously constructed apartments of 45 sq m for every member of the farmers' families, i.e. 50% larger than required. Now, if the farmer has four family members, they can choose to receive, say, one large 180 sq m (45x4) apartment or four apartments of 45 sq m each. With four apartments, they can choose to live in one and sell three away, realising a tidy capital sum, or keep them and lease them out. Each apartment can be leased for about RMB700 (US$89), and so with three they can get a monthly income of RMB2,100—an adequate income for the whole family! They don't have to work at all.

We visited the apartments and found the design practical and the finishings quite luxurious. Windows are double glazed to keep out the cold; they even have a large balcony space for *mahjong* (麻将), which the people in Chengdu simply love. It was a clever way to win hearts and minds. The farmers now have financial security and are housed in fashionable apartment. The outside landscape is equally beautiful.

When we were there I was told that the farmers were anxiously chasing for the handing over of their almost-ready apartments—they couldn't wait to move in—as this is such a sweet deal. Other farmers are clamouring for Zhixin to take over their farmland so that they can have similar benefits too!

Zhixin is indeed an innovative company. It makes similar deals with the local government for landbank. For example, it built a large, beautiful and stylish Flower Park, decorated with very modernistic sculptures, for the government to attract horticultural shows to the city. This promotes tourism, and in exchange Zhixin gets land. The company's residential projects are of very high-quality design—definitely not inferior to ours.

The company has a relatively young staff; even the chairman is barely 40 years old. It also has strong corporate governance and core value systems. It even runs its own school where new recruits learn about real estate as well as the core values of the group. The programme includes military-style training in uniform. Zhixin is entrepreneurial and yet also corporate in its thinking.

We gathered that a top US multinational was talking to Zhixin about a joint-venture too and that the CEO himself was personally involved in an attempt to win over the deal.

We signed the joint-venture after Yang Hao and his senior colleagues visited us, and we now have a landbank to build 25,000 affordable housing apartments in Chengdu with Zhixin.

As I said at the last staff communication session—don't think we are the best around. I believe we can learn from a Chengdu developer, too.

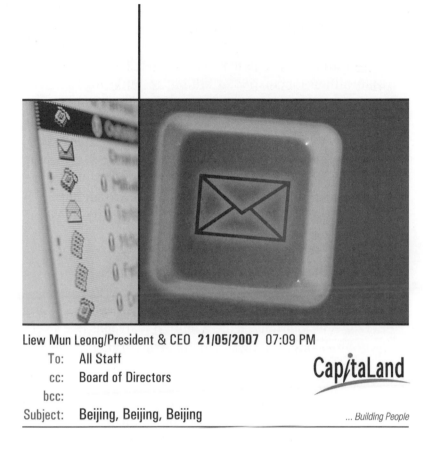

Liew Mun Leong/President & CEO **21/05/2007** 07:09 PM

To: All Staff

cc: Board of Directors

bcc:

Subject: **Beijing, Beijing, Beijing**

Cap/taLand

... Building People

B eijing is now feverishly preparing for next year's Olympic Games. It is only about 15 months away. Can Beijing do it, to make China proud? Many are sceptical. As for me, having first visited Beijing 25 years ago and seeing it now, and the progress it has made, I don't share the same scepticism.

BEIJING'S GREAT LEAP FORWARD

In a Harvard paper, the Dutch architect Rem Koolhaas has likened the urbanisation of the Pearl River Delta to the "Great Leap Forward". Beijing is now doing the same. Another author, Xing Ruan, describes the "unprecedented diversity of China's emerging new architecture" as "letting a hundred flowers blossom". Read on, and you may agree that this is happening in Beijing.

The Chinese government has budgeted to invest some RMB180 billion (about US$24 billion) to build up the city's infrastructure. They are taking this opportunity to rebuild and transform China's capital into a global city with completely new city and sport infrastructures and world-class buildings. These include a brand-new international airport designed by Norman Foster, a host of sport complexes and several iconic government buildings, all designed by renowned architects. A sample of these iconic designs as listed below will wow you, even before you visit Beijing to see them.

LET A HUNDRED FLOWERS BLOOM

(a) The Olympic National Stadium by Swiss architect firm Herzog & de Meuron – it has a rooftop that looks like a very busy bird's nest – a nightmare for structural engineers, or is it fun?

(b) The National Swimming Centre by PTW Architect – a large "watercube"- shaped building with a space frame that resembles a crystal cell molecular structure, clad with translucent ETFE[1] "pillows" similar to the "mushrooms" used on Clarke Quay's heat-reducing rooftop.

(c) The National Grand Theatre by Paul Andreu – a titanium-clad "eggshell" building that gracefully floats above a large man-made lake.

(d) The China Central Television (CCTV) HQ by Rem Koolhaas – two twin towers twisted to be connected at the top. Looks like an unstable structure designed for David Copperfield's escape act.

(e) The Beijing Books Building by Koolhaas & OMA – a large, intricate glass-block building with two "symbolic windows" purportedly to "channel" internal energy from the building to the street and plaza.

(f) The Sky Looped Hybrid Housing by Steven Holl — Eight high-rise residential towers linked as a loop in the sky like a street in the air. You can move from one tower to another without going down to street level.

ADVANCED DESIGN AND CONSTRUCTION TECHNOLOGY

I have visited the Olympic National Stadium and National Swimming Centre. Both are almost completed and are as beautiful as they have been designed to be. The contractors are local Chinese companies who have taken part in the very intricate structural design and formulated the necessary construction methodology. They have proven to have very advanced construction technology and project management techniques.

INVESTING IN DESIGN AND TALENTS

My message is that we have to invest in design and talents, wherever they may come from. Land costs in Beijing are much cheaper than Singapore in percentage terms. So in land-scarce Singapore, all the more we have to make sure that we create the most profitably designed buildings. And the most profitable buildings must come from the most creative designs. Beijing developers invest heavily to get the best designs, so that the best-value building can be created from their land. Believe me, celebrity "starchitects" are not cheap. I have worked with Frank Gehry and I should know—but I will also tell you he is worth every dollar.

How do we catch up in design, creativity and innovation? I am organising a design forum for our architects and designers next month in Shanghai to visit some of these iconic projects in Shanghai and Beijing. Seeing is believing. I think our designers will certainly be awed and inspired. We have to learn as fast as our Chinese peers or we will be left behind not only by Beijing, but also by many other inner cities in China. I just came back from Zhengzhou and Luoyang in Henan Province last week and boy, who says they're "inner cities"?!

SOFTWARE AND SERVICE IMPROVEMENT

But Beijing is not stopping at hardware alone. It is launching many programmes to train and upgrade the service industry to prepare for the large influx of foreign visitors to the Olympic Games. Beijing officials and even citizens are encouraged to learn English to help visitors when they move around in the city, and this is done with the help of volunteer teachers. Taxi drivers are required to learn English by masteering a few words every day. Hotels and restaurants are upgrading their services and public servants are instructed to be efficient and extra courteous. I visited Beijing two weeks ago and I did observe the city government and the community doing their best to prepare for the Olympic Games next year.

CUSTOMERS' IMMEDIATE ASSESSMENT

When I arrived at Beijing International Airport, I was greatly impressed (actually stunned) by the attempt to solve one of the perennial woes in many airports (both in developing and developed countries)—the immigration counter! (Forgive me for my lack of modesty, but I think Changi Airport, of which I'm the chairman, is a rare exception.) Guess what has been done? In front of the counter facing the visitors, there are four buttons for you, as a visitor, to rate the performance of the immigration officer attending to you. After he clears your passport, you can instantly rate his performance as "(i) Greatly Satisfied, (ii) Satisfied, (iii) Slow in Processing your passport, or (iv) Poor Customer Service". Talk about open-system assessment! This is a bold movement to implement for the public service. Apparently, this system is so successful that China Merchants Bank, which is already rated as one of the best retail banks in China, has also implemented this instant assessment system in its banking halls to improve retail banking services. Are we prepared to try this?

I'll tell you another development that Beijing is catching up on—shopping malls! CapitaLand now has 72 shopping malls in 25 cities in China, either already operating or under development. We are very proud of them. When you walk into one of them, whether it is in Chongqing or Hohhot in Inner Mongolia, they will have almost everything you can find in any supermarket in the US—and more. You can even find live eels and other exotic game food around. (I once saw a raw crocodile head for sale in a shopping mall!) Our malls in China are modern and sparklingly clean, well-managed and serving thousands of happy shoppers everyday.

Let me give you some comparisons. Several years ago I used to praise and idolise the Bluewater shopping mall in the UK. Developed by Lend Lease, I rated it as having overtaken the Mall of America in Minnesota, which I had a strong impression of when I visited. Not any more. On this last trip to Beijing, I stepped into a newly opened mall called Shin Kong Place (SKP) just opposite our Ascott serviced apartments in Beijing. The sophistication in this mall has exceeded all the shopping malls I have seen before. Some features of this 1.2 million sq ft (11,148 sq m) mall are as follows:

(a) The cosmetics section on the first floor that greets visitors when they enter the mall is very tastefully designed and charmingly lit up. Special rooms are centralised at the side for any demonstration or trial makeup so that customers do not have to sit around embarrassingly (unless you are an exhibitionist) like demonstration sale assistants if they wish to try something on.

(b) Luxuriously designed VIP and VVIP lounges are provided for high-end shoppers to try their intended purchases. High-end customers can try their garments, shoes, jewellery, watches, etc, in the private and luxurious comfort of a lounge (designed like an airline lounge), and they will be served with snacks, Champagne, a whole range of alcoholic drinks, fruits juices and hot beverages. Fitting rooms are very spacious and well-equipped with wide multi-angled mirrors for trial fitting. Doesn't fit? Not to worry. There is an alteration room with 20 tailors who can alter the garment for you within two hours. You can get a man's suit ready, perfectly fitted within 24 hours. The entire world's top-end fashion houses, e.g. LV, Prada, Gucci, and Dunhill, are there. I was told that in China, the fashion business is experiencing 25% to 30% growth. They are all very bullish, opening their outlets in China. Gucci, for example, is spending US$8 million to renovate its 150 sq m shop in this mall. Really irresistible!

(c) If you think this is over the top, look at what Panasonic is doing in this mall. It is now creating a 4,000 sq m showroom just to exhibit its products—household appliances, lifestyle, new technology, energy-saving products, the works. This is not for doing sales, just the largest showroom outside of Japan. Guess how much money they are spending? US$70 million! We can build a full-scale modern mall in China with that money. Obviously, the Japanese are putting big bets on China.

(d) I saw another unbelievable display of wealth in this mall. I was shown a bedsheet set consisting of bedsheets, blanket and two sets of pillow covers. They are supposed to be made from the best quality fine Egyptian cotton. I felt the cotton bedsheet. Indeed a silky smooth spread. The price tag: RMB1.2 million! Is there a buyer? Yes, three potential buyers.

I visited another shopping mall that I thought was ridiculous in idea and cost. Flanked by two four-storey buildings, a 30m by 300m LCD "screen" was erected on top like a flexible roof shelter to connect the two buildings. This rooftop screen can be used to generate colourful images or messages for advertisements. This roof screen alone costs

S$200 million (US$134 million). They can easily build a million-sq-m shopping mall with that money!

SERIOUS LESSONS

China is using the Olympic Games as an opportunity to showcase how it is transforming Beijing into a world-class cosmopolitan city. China certainly has bold ideas and it is seriously carrying them out. There are several lessons to learn from all these:

(a) Beijing is willing to hire foreign talents to design the landscape features of this ancient city. It is a bold and expensive move. China is open-minded to try it and prepared to pay for international design talents. At the same time, the local architects and designers can then learn from them. I had visited these international firms in the US and there are many Chinese architects working there. When all the pomp and fanfare for the Olympic Games are over, Beijing will have many iconic world-class buildings and its architects will have learnt lots from these "hundred flowers that have bloomed".

(b) China is willing to introduce drastic measures to improve its service industry, including its public service. I can't imagine how the immigration department and China Merchants Bank can persuade their colleagues to do instant and open customer surveys like those at the Beijing airport. I was told there are incentives for positive feedback. I also read that in Guangzhou, civil servants who receive more than six complaints will be fired. Someone wrote in the *China Daily* that six complaints are too many to tolerate, and it should be fewer. China is now very serious about improving, in both private and public services. Are we improving our services? I am concerned nowadays with the little details that are often overlooked by our colleagues. It is about discipline to follow the details.

(c) Beijing, Shanghai and other Chinese cities are investing in huge infrastructures and other development programmes to transform the cities. They have large land mass, now they have finance, and their business people are bold and entrepreneurial. If we don't move as fast, we will be in the backwaters. There is now fierce competition between global cities. Beijing, Shanghai, Guangzhou, Tokyo, Hong Kong, Bangkok. How do we fare?

Since 1982 I must have easily made more than one hundred trips to China, visiting gateway cities like Beijing, Shanghai and Guangzhou, traveling from the costal regions to the inner second- and third-tier cities in Yunnan, central China and the western-most regions in Xinjiang. Each and every trip never failed to surprise me with the progress that the Chinese are making. Quite frightening! How do we keep our distance ahead of them? Really, how much are we ahead of them? What is it that we have or can do that they don't have or can't do?

End Note

1 ETFE is ethylene tetrafluoroethylene, a fluorocarbon-based polymer (a kind of plastic), with high corrosion resistance and strength over a wide temperature range. An example of its use is as pneumatic panels to cover the outside of the football stadium Allianz Arena or the Beijing National Swimming Centre--the world's largest structure made of ETFE film (laminate).

Mr Liew Mun Leong/President & CEO **28/05/2007** 07:19 PM

To: All Staff

cc: Board of Directors

bcc:

Subject: **China's Happiest Place on Earth**

Cap/taLand

... Building People

You know we are now moving into the cities of inner China to expand our footprint there. We are established in Beijing, Shanghai and Guangzhou and recently have gone into Ningbo, Hangzhou and Foshan to develop residential projects. We are also managing and developing a total of 72 malls in 25 Chinese cities.

I spent last Friday and Saturday visiting Chengdu. At the airport whilst returning home, I told Lui Chong Chee[1] that each time I returned home from China I would, unfailingly, be awed by how China has progressed. Sometimes, I felt threatened with its overwhelming rate of progress and often asked whether we in Singapore would be left behind. I am not alone with this paranoia, I am sure.

Let me take this short two-day trip to Chengdu, as an example. But first, some salient points about Chengdu:

CITY PROFILE

Chengdu is the capital city of Sichuan Province, the political, cultural and economic hub of China's western region. It has a population of 10.8 million people and its GDP (gross domestic product) grew 13.5% in 2005. Its GDP per capita (2005) is US$2,739.

The major industries in Chengdu are IT (it is very much an IT hub, with the presence of tech giants like Intel, Motorola, IBM, Nokia), pharmaceuticals, food processing and mechanical engineering.

Chengdu has the largest immigrant population in China and its people strike one as having a *laissez-faire* attitude; they are easy going and enthusiastic consumers. It is not surprising that Chengdu is rated as the city with the highest happiness index in China.

PRO-BUSINESS GOVERNMENT

Chengdu's government is known to be very pro-business. I experienced this when meeting a district mayor there last year. I told her about our interest in developing a Raffles City in Chengdu, and how we had come across a suitable site in the city—the Sichuan Museum site.

I suggested that the site should have a link connection with the adjacent subway, which is now under construction. She said she would look into it as this would be under the subway authority's responsibility. Subsequently, the link connection proposal was approved.

Now for some good news. We bid against several local developers and two international bidders for the Sichuan Museum site—and we won.

We have engaged an internationally known "starchitect", Steven Holl, from the US, as our designer for this Raffles City Chengdu project. On this trip, Steven briefed me on his design, which consisted of a large retail mall, offices, two hotel buildings, serviced apartments and residential units, with a total gross floor area (GFA) of 2.5 million sq ft (232,257 sq m). It was an outstanding design, bold and bizarre. Its seven unique and mischievously-shaped buildings surround a large open public plaza to bring about the familiar feeling of New York's Rockefeller Center to Chengdu. We approved the design very quickly, but whilst watching the stunning model in front of me, I secretly lamented to myself that such an iconic building project should first be built in Chengdu—and not back home in Singapore. But never mind, it is still CapitaLand's project in Chengdu and we will be proud of it.

Another piece of good news: we successfully bid for a new site to build 3,800 homes.

As I arrived at the airport in Chengdu, Jason Leow[2] told me jubilantly that we had won a large residential site at a government auction. The site was secured at a very good price of RMB1.17 billion (US$156 million). It was also very nice to hear that within 10 minutes of the announcement, the party secretary telephoned our China CEO Lim Ming Yan[3] to thank him for the investment and invited him to a celebration lunch. Lim Ming Yan and Lui Chong Chee, who attended the lunch, complained to me that they should have brought along some "spare kidney capacity" for the lunch. (In short—they had to drink a lot!)

Like I said, the Chengdu government is evidently very pro-business.

I visited the site that day. It is indeed a lushly landscaped and beautiful site just off the third ring road, and next to the future district municipal government offices. Unencumbered, we can build 3,800 homes there in three phases. I am sure this will be another successful residential project in Chengdu.

A third piece of good news: our S$1 billion convertible bond. By late afternoon that day, we were told the wonderful news that our S$1 billion convertible bond had been oversubscribed more than two times within three hours of its launch. The deal also scored three record-breaking feats: the largest size in Asia (ex-Japan), the longest tenor, and the richest conversion premium of 72%.

It is simply wonderful to receive three pieces of good news in a day while in Chengdu.

ZHIXIN CAPITALAND JOINT VENTURE

Yang Hao, the chairman of our local partner Zhixin, briefed me about the progress of our Zhixin CapitaLand joint venture (JV). Our first JV project would be launched by this September and he spelt out how we would acquire several more large pieces of landbank. We toured the highly successful Floraland theme park, which was opened just last month. This theme park was developed with Samsung as the operation consultant (Samsung operates a very successful theme park called Everland in Korea) and Landmark (who designed many of Universal's rides, and are the creators of the Spider Man and Terminator 2 rides) as the creative consultant. Interestingly, Landmark's ride design typically costs US$1 million, but it was persuaded to do its R&D in Chengdu, resulting in a much cheaper cost. This has interested many suppliers who now want to source for these rides in Chengdu!

There were thousands of visitors at the park that day. The park was very well-kept and we could see cleaners in nice, smart uniforms gliding on roller skates to pick up litter. There were long queues at the rides, but the people didn't look unhappy about the long wait. One pull factor is that the park doesn't charge an admission fee—you just queue up and pay for each ride. I was told that the Chinese don't like the US model, where you have to pay large admission fees but get free rides throughout the park. They prefer to choose and pay for the rides that they like, and are prepared to queue even up to two hours, just for a couple of minutes of fun.

We walked through the completed housing project at the theme park. These are high-end, Spanish-design villas, townhouses and terraces. As we strolled along the estate, which is beautifully laid out and landscaped, we were treated to nice, piped-in classical music to enhance the experience. Of course the nice and gentle spring weather helped, but I must say that every detail has been thought through to make life much more relaxing there. Hence, Chengdu's high happiness index.

There is also a very sophisticated spa complex designed with all the requirements to provide complete relaxation. It was really very tempting to stay there longer. Everyone seemed to be having lots of fun. The Chengdu people already have their own integrated resort!

Well, after just another one-day tour of Chengdu, visiting the city centre, the theme park, the beautiful homes and staying at its five-star hotel and visualising the Raffles City that we're going to build, I can't help being awed by the progress there. Who says Chengdu is an "inner city"?

End Notes

1 Lui Chong Chee is CEO, CapitaLand Residential Limited.
2 Jason Leow is Deputy CEO, CapitaLand China Holdings Pte Limited.
3. Lim Ming Yan is the CEO of CapitaLand China Holdings, a subsidiary of CapitaLand Residenial.

Chapter 5

Inspiring Encounters

"Leading is everything. There is no excuse!"

"You don't have to decide everything. Let go. But know what is happening. Stay on top."

I have visited many cities for business, and I've met all sorts of interesting and inspiring people, from business tycoons and government officials to artists and everyday Joes.

Some show courage against adversity, others great business acumen.

But though they may lead very diverse lives, they often have one common thread: they always persevere and are extremely focused.

I have found great inspiration from older, already very successful businessmen who still have the drive and energy to continue working. They could retire and enjoy the fruits of their labour, but instead they continue to work at the top of their game pursuing their passion with a strong zeal and interest in life. I have met several great "white hairs" who are of great inspiration to me. Even at the age of 80, they are still a bundle of energy. As one said to me: "Don't tell me your age. Tell me your energy."

There is something great in them that one can reflect on and learn from. Each encounter is interesting; just having a chat with them can teach us so much, not only in business, but also in life.

As one Chinese saying goes, "If you have an elder at home, you have a treasure for the family" (家有一老，如有一宝). Let's keep the treasure, but we must respect them. We will become one some day.

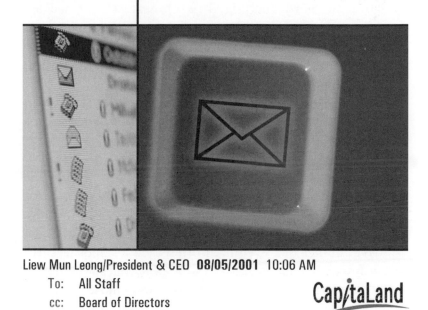

Liew Mun Leong/President & CEO **08/05/2001** 10:06 AM

To: All Staff

cc: Board of Directors

bcc:

Subject: **Patriotism Pays**

CapitaLand

... Building People

I had a nostalgic meeting in Hong Kong yesterday. Besides its sentimentality, it answered the question "Does patriotism pay?" Not obvious in these modern days of personal wealth seeking?

Twelve years ago, in 1989, I went around the US and Europe with the EDB[1] to recruit Chinese engineers and scientists who were then studying for their doctorates at renowned universities such as Cambridge, Oxford, Harvard and the Massachusetts Institute of Technology. Recruiting foreign talent for Singapore had started in the wake of a grave shortage of researchers for our national science and technology drive.

147

It was a good "harvest" and I headhunted more than 50 top Chinese scientists and engineers for SISIR.[2] One of them, a bright computer engineer Wang Ming, recommended that I recruit his personal friend and former roommate in the UK, by the name of Fu Yu Ning. This Chinese scholar had left London University immediately after his PhD to return to China to work. It was then just after the June 4th Tiananmen Square student crackdown and I recognised it as the best time to "steal" talent from China.

I journeyed to Shekou (a quiet logistics base near Shenzhen) to meet Fu in a rather dingy Chinese restaurant. We chatted the whole night and quickly seemed to get along well. He was then working in a shipping logistics base—a joint-venture operation between China Merchants and Sembawang Corporation.[3] China Merchants was formed more than 100 years ago during the Qing dynasty and is still one of the most successful international state-owned enterprises in China.

Over dinner that evening, I offered Fu a senior research fellowship in Singapore with a salary many times what he was getting then. Don't forget, in the late '80s, salaries in China were meagre and conditions were hard and unpromising, especially after the Tiananmen Square episode. Tacit in my offer was also Singapore citizenship for himself and his family—a very cherished and sought-after offer for many Chinese then. Confidence was then at the lowest point and many Westerners were sure Tiananmen Square would be the end of modernisation and reform in China. Many forecasted a downfall, and that widespread chaos would befall the country. Who would not jump at my offer?

To my surprise, Fu politely turned me down—he told me that it was fate that he had returned to China at that unfortunate time. But he would stay behind to help the country. The "country needs me" he said proudly, and he would not abandon his country because of the current political unrest. I thought he was naive, but was very touched. I also sensed that I could not change his decision, but told him that I would always welcome him if he ever wished to reconsider the offer. I knew then that this was a man to watch. Over the next couple of years we stayed in touch, but thereafter lost contact with each other for almost 10 years.

Recently Sembawang Corporation CEO Wong Kok Siew brought Fu to meet Ho Ching. Guess what, he is now president of China Merchants Group—a large conglomerate of shipping, logistics, banking (sixth-largest bank in China), insurance, technology and property. It is one of Sembawang's most important business clients. Fu told Ho Ching that he knew me and that I had bought a Beijing property from China Merchants at a rock-bottom price. Which is true—we bought two apartment blocks (400 units to be turned into serviced apartments) at a very low price. It had taken three rounds of negotiation over three years, but I bargained the price down from US$2,500 per square metre to US$1,240 per square metre. Every time the negotiations broke down, I warned them that at the next round I would reduce my offer price and I stuck to that threat until they finally yielded last year.

I was elated to hear of Fu's rise through the ranks to be the president of the group. Although we hadn't met for almost 10 years, he reminded me of the fire sale in Beijing, which fortunately he had not been involved in then. He joked that after so many years, I looked the same but he had aged quite a bit. He is 10 years younger than me and I congratulated him that at 44, he has done extremely well to be head of such a large Chinese enterprise. I observed that nowadays, it is common to find my Chinese counterparts younger than me— the Chinese have rightly given up on "seniority over talent and meritocracy".

We talked of old times and I reminded him that I could still remember his PhD thesis on vibration and of how I had wanted him to start a vibration laboratory for me in SISIR. Luckily for him I guess, he didn't accept my offer. We briefed each other on our business scope and readily agreed to explore possible collaboration. We parted feeling nostalgic and surprised at the event that brought us together again.

The world is small, or is it fate? We exchanged mobile phone numbers to make sure that we remain contactable.

Fu was patriotic, worked hard and persevered to serve his country during its most uncertain and turbulent days. He has been rewarded and he deserves it. Patriotism pays. But how many of us in Singapore would truly stay behind to take a similar bet, I wonder?

End Notes

1 EDB is the Economic Development Board of Singapore.
2 SISIR refers to the Singapore Institute of Standards and Industrial Research, a statutory board responsible for Singapore's national standards and industrial research and development to support the manufacturing industry in Singapore. Liew Mun Leong was CEO of SISIR for five years.
3 Sembawang Corporation is a government-linked conglomerate in Singapore.

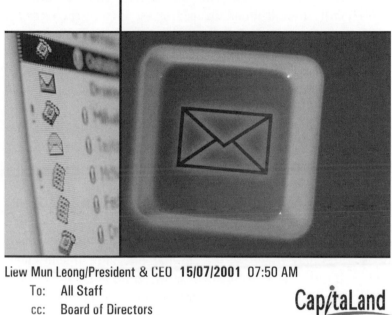

Liew Mun Leong/President & CEO **15/07/2001** 07:50 AM

To: All Staff

cc: Board of Directors

bcc:

Subject: **The Golfing Blind Man**

Cap/taLand

... Building People

I will tell you a remarkable and inspiring story of someone I heard about who lives life as usual even after a very severe personal setback.

Last month, I met Derek Clark (one of our UK Pidemco Land retirees) and he told me that he has been enjoying life playing lots of golf. Now golf is the world's most difficult ball sport. It requires the perfect co-ordination of no less than six body movements from the feet, knees, hips, arms, hands and head together, with full focus and fixation of our eyes. It requires total and undivided mental concentration if you want to hit the ball right. A slight distraction or misstep and your ball will fly to just where you don't want it to go. It involves life-long learning, and even a good player will still occasionally look like an idiot bashing the innocent ground when he does an "air shot".

I started playing 12 years ago, gave it up for 10 years and recently took it up again to destress during the extreme tense period of the DBS Land/Pidemco Land merger. I still play very badly as I don't play often enough to really learn the fundamentals well. But I console myself that it is a strange, unnatural sport (you play with your left hand) and that I have started late in life. Although I jog and exercise regularly, frequently my body movements are too stiff and I am not agile enough to have a well-co-ordinated swing. But I believe in the suggestion that in golf—unlike other sports—you don't have to be good at it to enjoy it.

I played one round with Derek and as usual I played poorly (still in triple digits—a beginner's scorecard). He tried to encourage me by telling me a very inspiring story. Recently he met and played golf with a 75-year-old English gentleman who is blind! I was astonished! How could someone who is blind play golf? Although the ball is static (as compared to a moving ball in other games like tennis or football), it is very difficult to hit it squarely.

This man used to run a sports shop in the UK, but unfortunately in 1976 he was involved in a traffic accident that resulted in him becoming blind. He was then 40 years old and in his prime. Badly hurt, he was hospitalised for many months. But he didn't give up and continued with his life, running the sports shop and continuing to play golf. I thought that was very brave and he must have extremely strong will power to live life that way. And guess what—he is the secretary of the Association of Blind Golfers, which shows that he's not the only one!

Is it golf that is so overwhelmingly addictive or is it his very strong determination and perseverance to live and enjoy life despite such a severe setback? Are you inspired? Many CEOs and top executives can't hit a stationary ball well with all their able bodies, sharp eyes and full concentration! It is humiliating, but also challenging, to these people who think they can move the whole world but sometimes cannot move a small ball.

Lesson: Don't give up easily on life, even when the most difficult times hit you. As long as you are alive, live to the fullest!

Liew Mun Leong/President & CEO **24/09/2003** 04:53 PM

To:	All Staff
cc:	Board of Directors
bcc:	
Subject:	**Pearls of Wisdom**

Cap/taLand

... Building People

I am going to start a new series of emails called "Take With You". They contain inspiring comments, views and statements I have heard in my conversations with the various clever people I have met; statements that we can reflect on and learn from.

From Masamoto Yashiro, chairman & CEO of Shinsei Bank, over lunch: "When I look at a person I don't look at his age. I look at his energy level."

From Hernando de Soto (Peruvian author of *The Mystery of Capital*) at the Forbes Global Conference in Shanghai, "Do you know why there are so many people of Japanese origin in Brazil and Peru now? Because Brazil and Peru were much richer than Japan in the 1930s and the Japanese went there to make a living!"

And de Soto quoting Albert Einstein: "How much does the fish know about the water it swims in?"

From Kenneth Chenault, chairman & CEO, American Express Co, quoting Napoleon: "Leadership is about defining reality and giving hope."

From Albert Yee, chairman of Yee Associates (famous structural engineer in the US): "Most people degenerate with age. We should regenerate instead."

Take these pearls of wisdom with you.

Liew Mun Leong/President & CEO **12/01/2004** 08:57 PM

To:	All Staff
cc:	Board of Directors
bcc:	
Subject:	*Sake*, Anyone?

Cap/taLand

... Building People

I want to start the New Year by writing on "Commitment". How far can we go?

Commitment to the company, said Wee Cho Yaw, chairman of UOB,[1] is as important as capability and integrity. "It is no use having a capable and honest man if he is not committed to his company", he told me recently. I cannot agree more. If you are not committed, you can't do your job well—simple statement of fact.

Recently, I chanced upon a Discovery Channel documentary that dramatically illustrated the highest level of commitment a man could give to his cause. Entitled *The Divine Wind*, it is fascinating, moving and utterly inspirational.

It was set in October 1944, when the American forces were launching a fierce naval attack on the Philippines. The Germans were on the verge of losing the war in Europe after the Allied forces successfully landed in Normandy. The Japanese had to defend desperately their last military stronghold in the Far East. It was going to be the last big battle.

The attacking US Fleet, consisting of the then very sophisticated aircraft carriers, was formidable, even though in those days, guided missiles and "smart bombs" were not invented yet. The Japanese fighter pilots had to fire more than four or five bombs to get a successful hit and still might not destroy or damage the ship badly. Their military resources were running dangerously low. The US assault had to be stopped at all costs. The Japanese air force commander madly came up with a desperate military strategy—"one aircraft hit must destroy one enemy ship"—to be executed by *kamikaze* (divine wind) suicide fighter pilots crashing their aircrafts into the enemy ship.

He asked for volunteers from an air squadron that consisted of unmarried fighter pilots.

There were only two rewards for the volunteers:

(1) Just before the deadly mission, they would be served with a cup of *sake* (Japanese rice wine) bestowed by the emperor.

(2) A promise of a memorial place—together with other *kamikaze* pilots—in a shrine blessed by the emperor.

All volunteered!

The black and white Discovery Channel documentary showed a film of four *kamikaze* pilots drinking the honoured *sake*, saluting the commander, uttering to one another, "See you at the Shrine", and marching off bravely (or was it recklessly?) to deliver their final commitment. Their greatest fear was not to die in this last mission. The commander's last instruction to them was, "Come back dead".

This aviation equivalent of hand-to-hand combat was highly debilitating for the US forces. Many ships were destroyed and the threat was frighteningly unstoppable. Ironically, the *kamikaze* pilots were deeply feared and admired by their enemy for such high order of courage and total commitment. American soldiers were seen respectfully lowering failed *kamikaze* pilots in coffins wrapped with American flags into the deep blue sea.

Touching! To be saluted this way must be the ultimate mark of respect that an enemy can give you, don't you think?

So serious was the threat of the "divine wind" that back in the US, news of such a devastating military tactic by the enemy was banned. It would cause a panic and loss of morale by the forces.

Letters were written by family members of the *kamikaze* pilots to extol their bravery, loyalty and commitment to the country's war. One mother wrote, "You are my son, but you are not my son. You are the son of the emperor."

The story of *kamikaze* pilots marked a new chapter in modern military history and it dramatically demonstrated the spirit and highest possible order of commitment to a man's cause.

Such acts of honour and bravery are quite common in Japan's culture and history—they manifest themselves in different forms and in different times. In modern Japan, as late as in the '70s and '80s, we still witnessed suicide attempts by Japanese executives to bear total responsibility for their business mistakes or failures.

I am not about to suggest we suddenly all turn into *kamikaze* pilots—definitely not quite necessary in our corporate world. But how far would we go in our commitment? You tell me; I have some *sake* too!

End Note

1 UOB is United Overseas Bank, a leading bank in Singapore and a dominant player in the Asia Pacific.

Liew Mun Leong/President & CEO **28/06/2004** 04:43 PM

To: All Staff

cc: Board of Directors

bcc:

Subject: **Octogenarian Wisdom**

Cap/taLand

... Building People

Recently I was introduced to a very inspiring and visionary businessman who had conceived and undertaken many ambitious building projects.

S P Tao is 88-years-old—a Singapore property veteran who pioneered development projects from the early 1960s to 1980s, two generations and many property cycles ahead of us. He founded Singapore Land (SingLand) in the '60s, and he is credited with many of Singapore's landmark buildings, e.g. Clifford House, Shell Tower, Gateway and Marina Square. He was also a shipping tycoon.

I had never met him personally and therefore readily accepted his surprise request for a meeting. He came alone without any staff entourage. And he walked from his office in Shing Kwan House in Shenton Way to Capital Tower. After a short introduction, he meticulously rattled off the details of a proposed project in Nanjing, all from memory and without any reference materials. His clarity, passion and persuasion would easily put many MBA yuppies to shame. How could anyone say no to him? I agreed to take a look!

Over the next few days, he called me on my mobile directly to discuss arrangements to visit the site. Not long after, Tham Kui Seng, Lim Ming Yan and I were busily trotting around on the 40-hectare site with him, followed by meetings with the landowner, and city and provincial officials. He was a tireless marketer and remember, he was 88!

Everyone in Nanjing was very respectful to him and with good reason. As early as 1983 he built the Jinling Hotel, which at 37 storeys (that was his lucky number) was the tallest and also the first five-star hotel in his hometown of Nanjing. The hotel was then arguably the most modern in the whole of China.

That same year, I had made my first trip to China, which was just opening its doors to international visitors, and I had stayed in the Jin lin Hotel for one night. I remember the hotel being constantly surrounded by hundreds of curious locals staring in disbelief at the ultra-modern building. The hotel management generously conducted tours of the premises for the crowd, who had never been into such a modern building before. I vividly remember how a young Chinese girl in the elevator suddenly screamed and passed out—she couldn't take the shock of the vertical motion! Some interesting remarks from S P Tao:

On how he kept himself so well and energetic at 88:

"There are two things I don't go after: money and fame. So I do what I like."

I think he has lots of both already!

On how he came to Singapore:

"In the early '60s I decided to migrate from Burma to either Hong Kong or Singapore, two cities where there were many Chinese people. Then, I found that there were only two kinds of people in Hong Kong—those who look up to you and those who look down on you. Singapore was much more equal."

On his three guiding principles for doing property business:

"Forty years ago we started SingLand and my friend in Hong Kong Land told me about three guiding principles: investment is for growth, trading is for profit and management fees are for management. I still remember these three principles today."

These sound very much like CapitaLand's strategies too—except the last one!

On doing business:

"In business, you have to take the initiative, execute and then follow through until the end. I never, never give up, no matter how tough it gets. Execution is very important, but first you must make a decision. One of my very brilliant aides (a Harvard MBA scholar) always asked me 'Mr Tao what shall we do now?' I asked him: 'What do you want to do?' He never decides on anything and never succeeds in anything."

On his personal assistants:

"There is a Chinese saying that you need four good assistants— like your two hands and two legs. But your head must be firmly on your body controlling your two hands and two legs."

Sounds like China's "Gang of Four" during the cultural revolution—if the head is not controlling "the four" they will get out of control eventually!

Kui Seng, Ming Yan and I thoroughly enjoyed meeting this highly energetic octogenarian. With his rich experiences, he is witty, still full of drive and loves life. He labelled himself as "lao Nanjing" (老南京) or "old Nanjing" and fondly called me his "xiao di di" (小弟弟) or "little brother", which I gladly acknowledged.

How could I argue when he is three decades ahead of me and still a bundle of energy? Whatever his background or history, he certainly is a great inspiration!

Liew Mun Leong/President & CEO **15/10/2004** 05:03 PM

To: All Staff
cc: Board of Directors
bcc:
Subject: **Wynn-ing Details**

Cap/taLand

... Building People

S teve Wynn is one of the most famous developers in Las Vegas. His legendary projects there include world-famous landmarks such as Treasure Island, the Mirage, and more recently the Bellagio—all high-end, integrated entertainment, gaming, convention, and hotel developments that help to bring in the 35 million visitors that come to the "four-mile strip" in Vegas every year. Each of these multi-billion US-dollar developments is easily a few million square feet in scale—overwhelming, gigantic, grand and flashy.

They are all so highly sought after by tourists that he has cleverly sold them one by one to his rivals in the city.

I met Steve last week in New York and he invited me

to visit his current project in Las Vegas, which is now in an advanced stage of construction. Of course, I agreed to go and I learnt a lot from him during this visit.

It is a magnificent and stunning project. Eventually, the 8 million sq ft (743,224 sq m) development will have more than 4,000 hotel rooms, a few hundred thousand square feet of convention space, beautifully designed theatres and upmarket restaurants, and retail space for all the world's top-branded products including Ferrari cars, and not forgetting the cutting-edge gaming halls—all surrounded by man-made mountains with real trees and greenery, and towering water fountains.

What amazed me most was that Steve knew literally every inch of this mega project. He passionately related to me every little detail of design and construction when he showed us around the project (scheduled completion is April 2005). He knew virtually every nook and cranny of the layout: its dimensions, materials used down to little things like the thread count of the bedsheets and varieties of shrubbery planted. He even told me about the special lifting equipment the contractor used—how long the lifting arms were, the counterweights and operating characteristics. This attention to detail is all the more admirable given the fact that he is slightly visually impaired and has to be assisted when walking around parts of the site. The scaffolding, the construction machines and debris here and there did not deter or bother him!

Some reflections:

(1) Why would a man in his 60s who has done so much—he must have developed more than 30 million sq ft of projects worth tens of billions of dollars, and he must be personally worth billions of dollars—still strive so hard and be so passionate about his work? His fighting spirit and passion keep burning. It is his love for his creations—it is what they call a "labour of love".

(2) Despite his position, he retains a remarkable penchant for, and focus on, details. He is very hands-on. Many Singaporeans in his position would have delegated such details to others to follow through. They are not hands-on and don't know much of the details of what is going on. Careless mistakes can crop up frequently and this will leave them helpless. How can we develop operational excellence and develop a Singapore brand for our products or services this way?

(3) Steve has built three great entertainment complexes, and each time, he has made changes to improve on the previous project. In fact, for this current one, he has reversed certain design philosophies, e.g. building the main attraction like the volcanoes and pirates' ship inside the complex rather than outside, building a hotel within a hotel, shortening walking distances, etc. It demonstrates that in development we need to go through experiences after experiences to remain at the forefront. We just can't jump in with money, hire some world-class architects and consultants and suddenly become a world-class, big-time developer. We need to really understand what it takes to evolve concepts, designs and operations.

Unlike manufacturing a product, each of our projects is on a different piece of land, which will make it unique and different. To be a great developer, it is not enough to be able to read economic cycles, secure good land at good prices and speculate on demand.

We need financial discipline, but we also need to have strong vision, creativity, boldness and passion to create and to correct past mistakes.

Can we take on such big undertakings in Singapore and help bring in 35 million tourists and all the related economic spin-offs to the country, and of course make money? Do we have the qualities to be such a great, visionary developer?

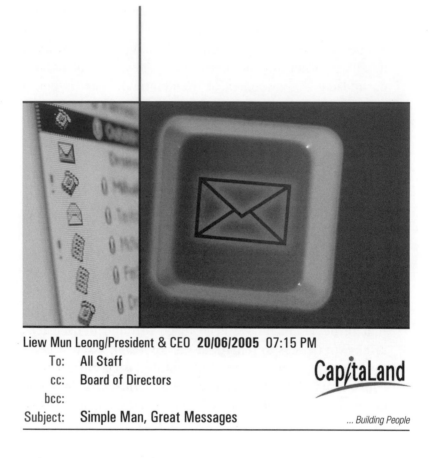

Liew Mun Leong/President & CEO **20/06/2005** 07:15 PM

To: All Staff

cc: Board of Directors

bcc:

Subject: **Simple Man, Great Messages**

CapitaLand

... Building People

My late father was a poor, Chinese immigrant who had to leave his impoverished village home in China in the early 1900s to seek a living. He was a simple man who gave us simple advice, but his words have turned out to be great lessons in life for us. Let me recollect some of the words of wisdom that he tried to impart to my siblings and me:

(a) "Study hard son, so that when you grow up you can work under a ceiling fan." He aspired to give us a good education so that we could have a better life than him. In those days (in the '60s) only white-collar workers, like clerks and above, could work in the luxury of an office with a ceiling fan. His ceiling fan wish sounded like a great ambition then and we were inspired! When I graduated in 1970 I worked at Singapore's Ministry of Defence at Pearl's Hill, and I was privileged to have an office with a ceiling fan!

(b) "Son, don't just be a doorstep barking dog. Go further from home and make it there." He challenged us to brave the unknown, to go beyond our comfort zone. Was he already hinting to us to go overseas then? He had to—for survival, he left China!

(c) "If your head is not so big, son, don't try to wear that big hat." He reminded us that whilst we should be ambitious about taking bigger challenges, we should not go beyond our real capabilities. However, in my view, if we feel we have more potential, we should aim to wear a larger hat. Just make sure it's not wishful thinking and that you can carry its size and weight; but please, don't allow your head to swell and get carried away!

(d) "Son, there is no such thing as an unwanted fat goose running on the street for you to take." The English equivalent might be "Don't be naive. There is no such thing as a free lunch", or "There is nothing in the world that is both free and good—not even cheap and good", I think.

Simple messages from a simple man, but these are some great lessons that guide my life and the best gifts I received from my father. He was a great teacher, a great father!

Happy Father's Day!

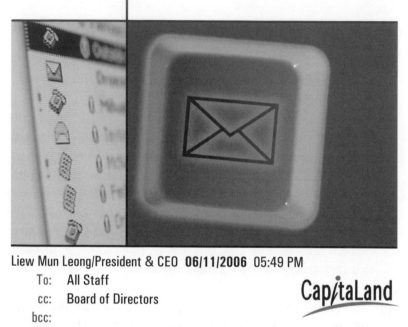

Liew Mun Leong/President & CEO **06/11/2006** 05:49 PM

To: All Staff

cc: Board of Directors

bcc:

Subject: **An Entrepreneur—A Man of Steel**

Cap/taLand

... Building People

I used to say that if you think you are a great CEO or leader, try leading a difficult company or an organisation or country in bad times. Recently, I have come to realise that a much greater test of leadership is when a leader still has to lead in the face of a sudden, severe personal crisis or tragedy. I witnessed this test thrown cruelly at Sol Kerzner, the chairman and founder of Kerzner International following the tragic death of Butch Kerzner, who was not only Sol's eldest son, but also the CEO of Kerzner International.

Kerzner International is our leading partner (60:40 partnership) for the Sentosa Integrated Resort (IR) bid. We are all aware that this is indeed a very competitive and combative bid. We have worked for two years with Sol and Butch. We chose them as partners because of their experience and track record as a world-class resort developer. They developed Sun City in South Africa, their home country; Atlantis in the Bahamas; the United States' second-largest casino, Mohegan Sun, in Connecticut; and are now building another Atlantis IR in Dubai. They want the Sentosa IR to be Asia's best resort, their Asian showpiece.

The Kerzners are very intense people—entrepreneurial, bold and highly creative. They have a strong management team and are excellent partners. After two years of hard work together and with the top-class design from world-renowned star architect Frank Gehry, we were all prepared to present our proposal to the ministerial committee on October 16th. We knew it was going to be a tough fight and this time round we had taken every competitor seriously.

But tragedy struck and Sol showed his mettle, not only as an entrepreneur but also as a man of steel.

I will tell you what I witnessed: On October 11th I was attending a dinner in New York's Mandarin Oriental Hotel where Singapore's Minister Mentor Lee Kuan Yew was being awarded the highly regarded Woodrow Wilson Award. Three quarters of the way through the dinner I went to the restroom and at the same time, switched on my handphone to check for messages. Sok Kheng had left an urgent message: "Please call back urgently". I called back straight away and was told the unbelievably tragic news. Sol had called to inform me that Butch had died in a helicopter accident flying across the Dominican Republic, while spotting for new resort sites. I was stunned and took a moment to recover before asking for Sol's contact number.

I went back to the dinner in a daze, still trying to accept the tragic news. I had worked with Butch for two years on the IR project, wrestling and sometimes fighting with him over ideas. At 42, Butch was bright, young and a promising CEO with an MBA degree from Stanford. He had worked as an investment banker on Wall Street and later joined his dad, eventually rising to become the company's CEO.

Many past events and questions raced across my mind as I pondered the consequences of the tragedy. How could I console the family? I couldn't help wondering how it would affect our project. Would Sol lose interest in the project, or worse, but understandably, abandon us and pull out?

Soon after dinner I quietly slipped to my hotel room to call Sol. I sat down for a long time trying hard to figure out how to broach the tragic topic with him. After a long hesitation, I plucked up enough courage and called him. He was in London. I offered my deepest condolences. He was composed and said to me, "I think Butch would want us to carry on with the presentation. I will come to Singapore on Sunday to meet you."

I was very touched by his words of assurance and commitment. I had expected him to say that he wouldn't travel to Singapore. It would have been perfectly understandable. In fact, I suggested that he spend time with Butch's family. I assured him that we and his very able senior colleagues could handle the presentation. But he was firm and insisted that he would fly in on Sunday for the presentation immediately after the funeral.

As expected, there was wide speculation that Sol would not turn up and that we had lost our head for the fight. Sol proved the rumours wrong. He came to lead the presentation and we put on a good show.

At the presentation, Deputy Prime Minister S Jayakumar kindly offered his condolences when meeting Sol. He was again composed and led the presentation ably. However, he couldn't totally hide his emotions as he constantly referred to Butch as "his boy" who did this and that. The last video show that we had prepared before with sound bites and comments from all of us was difficult to manage. Butch was the last one to make a comment and his very last statement was that he believed Atlantis Sentosa would be a huge success "long after we are gone". Sol was choked with tears, but we hadn't had time to erase that rather unfortunate if prophetic statement in the video.

After the presentation, at about 7pm, Sol bravely suggested that we conduct an unplanned press conference. We had not prepared for this, but agreed to his surprise request. After that press conference, in which he appeared calm and unaffected, we bade each other goodbye and he immediately flew back to London.

Two nights ago, Sol called me to make an arrangement to meet again in New York the following week to prepare for our next round of presentations to the permanent secretary committee on November 29th. He sounded strong and very encouraging.

I think only a man of steel could have conducted himself that way, when, even in the face of the tragic death of his son and business colleague, he could harness enough courage, calm and determination to go forward with the IR competition in Sentosa. I am sure he must have cried a lot at home and probably in solitude for the loss of "his boy", but this senior entrepreneur could still brave the world of business to show that he is unscathed by such a personal tragic loss of a loved one. Many would not be able to withstand such sudden pain and would have given up.

I have learnt a lot about life, leadership and commitment from a partner who has suffered so much. Whether we are eventually successful in the bid or not, I salute this "Man of Steel".

Chapter 6

Of Business
and Ethics

"You may be very capable, but your value system will decide your growth potential or limitation. It will be your career ceiling."

I was a struggling young man on my first job when one day, an envelope containing a large sum of money mysteriously appeared on my desk. Surprised, I asked the people around the office, offering to return the money to its rightful owner. Little did I know that the envelope was actually a test of my integrity by my new boss! He had planted the envelope with the money in it.

The property development industry is packed full of multi-million dollar contracts and opportunities abound for kickbacks. CapitaLand's strict principle has always been "if we have to bribe, we won't do the business", because I believe one can establish a relationship with partners and governments in a sincere, meaningful way without bribery.

CSR (corporate social responsibility) needs to be more than buzzwords on a corporate document, and I think the first thing any socially responsible multinational must do in a developing country is not to indulge in bribery and corruption, even if it is "local business practice". I strongly believe that it is morally irresponsible to bribe the society where we conduct our business. It will destroy the very moral fabric of the society. Recently, I discussed this in a Harvard China Review conference at Harvard University. I stressed this point to send the message to the bright Chinese students there, that corruption must not be taken as a normal way of doing business in China.

I have always had zero tolerance for corruption and will deal very seriously with any bribery discovered, however small.

But integrity is more than incorruptibility and absolute honesty. For me, the concept also incorporates the attributes of courage and doing what is right, and is about responsibility, accountability, justice, openness and humility.

Business ethics are very important to building up the brand of a company. If its reputation and image are not impeccable, the company's bottom line will suffer and eventually not survive. To become the partner of choice, you must observe strict business ethics.

I want CapitaLand's name to stand for fairness towards all its stakeholders—not only towards its shareholders, but also its employees and its partners. I often tell our partners "we won't make money out of you, and you shouldn't make money out of us. We should make money together from the market".

I have also warned our colleagues that we can take market

or business risk, but we should never take reputation risk. We can lose money and later make it back. We cannot do the same with our reputation.

Liew Mun Leong/President & CEO **21/09/1998** 07:35 AM

To: All Staff

cc: Board of Directors

bcc:

Subject: **Don't Take Everything from the Table**

Cap/taLand

... Building People

E arning a reputation for fair and honest business dealings is important for us to compete internationally. If we are well-known for our fair and equitable deals—be it selling condominiums; renting hotel rooms; leasing serviced apartments, retail space and offices; offering property management services; or forming a joint-venture—then our buyers, customers or business associates will have confidence in us and come back on a long-term basis. They will come back because they have experienced good deals and have benefited from dealing with us!

Easier to say than to fully understand and do. Let's say we are negotiating a joint-venture deal. Some of us may want to maximise our position by "taking everything from the table". This is a short-term, transactional approach. We can't build long-term business relationships this way. I prefer "optimisation" on a win-win basis, generating long-term benefits for both sides. If everyone tries to maximise everything for himself, then one party may suffer, and even if he gives in there will be misgivings, resulting in a win-lose situation and finally, a break-up. Offer best value to our customers or partners and they will cherish a long-term relationship with us. Sounds simple, but in driving a deal, we need to be very balanced in our positioning. We don't need to be greedy!

The above is especially important in joint-venture negotiations. There is often a wrong perception in the business community that government-linked companies (GLCs) will always take advantage of their position as a "big brother", with the government behind them.

I learnt of someone from a GLC who wished to work with a small local company, but his first sentence on the phone was: "We want to buy over your company." The owner of that small company was instantly offended and put off. To him, it was a typical GLC throwing its weight around. The potential partner would feel that the obnoxious GLC manager was naive and did not know how business is done. What made the person at the GLC think that the owner would like to sell his company to a GLC or let a large share of his company go? Just because he represents a GLC and has asked for involvement in his company? Well, while some companies may get frightened away, others may think, "Let's rip off these naive GLC people and take them for a ride".

I read somewhere that the government is like a hippopotamus. It is big, fat, and while it may be comfortable to go to bed with, when it rolls over you, you will be finished! Many companies are suspicious that we, as a GLC, will roll over on them. But let's not forget that the hippo can also be asleep sometimes and his partner may be using this big animal to warm him up and add to his balance sheet!

Some myths about GLCs:

a) GLCs must subsidise them. For example, some executive condominium (EC) buyers still think we are like HDB giving out subsidies and freebies. No, we are neither the HDB nor a statutory board.

b) GLCs should not make a profit. OK, we don't grab unfair profit from a sale or deal, but as a business we must be profitable to grow the company. We do need to make a decent level of profit like any other commercial enterprise. My first lesson in business class was "the only reason why a business exists is to make profit". Not totally, but largely true!

c) GLCs are run by ex-civil servants and can be ripped off. Not true! Many of us may have civil service backgrounds. Yes, the civil service is orderly, structured and systematic in training its staff, but this does not stop civil servants or former civil servants from smelling a rotten deal when there is one. Besides, many of us have had a stint in the commercial world, dealing with both angels and devils before! When I first took over L&M,[1] the people there were apprehensive that I may turn it into a government department since I came from supposedly "angelic" places like PWD and SISIR! Yes, I introduced systems and accountability and promoted integrity, but we were just as commercial-minded and profit-driven.

d) If the GLC doesn't agree on the deal, then run to the government to complain. So far, my experience is that the government, as our shareholder, doesn't intervene unless we have been unfair or wrong. GLCs are not run as an extension of the government ministries or statutory boards! They are commercial companies and not government departments. They have their own independent management and board of directors. They can be sued or sue; they can make money or be made bankrupt.

Message:

- Be fair, firm and reasonable in our commercial dealings. Think of the long term with our customers, clients or business partners. We must be honourable and deliver what we promise. HONOUR is important! There is a Chinese saying that "whatever promises from our mouths are as good as gold" (牙齿当金使).

- Don't take everything from the table. Leave something for your partners, too. I always tell my partners that they should never make money from me and I won't make money from them; the market is out there and we can both make money together.

- As a GLC, don't give the wrong impression to others. We shall be honourable, but we must be commercial and smart at the same time. Sometimes we need to show them that we mean business. Can you do that?

End Note

1 L&M is a public listed engineering and construction company in Singapore, which Liew Mun Leong headed for several years.

Liew Mun Leong/President & CEO **03/06/2001** 07:00 PM

To: All Staff

cc: Board of Directors

bcc:

Subject: **A Lesson from Angkor Wat**

Cap/taLand

... Building People

L ast month, I visited our two hotels in Cambodia and had the chance to tour Phnom Penh and Siem Reap, the world-famous temples and the infamous "killing fields". Richard Helfer assured me that it is now a safe tourist place to go. I was greatly affected by some memorable graphic impressions that I tried to moralise one way or another— but not without depressing sentiments and emotions. On return, I kept encouraging everyone to visit Cambodia to experience these extraordinary places and for some eye-opening lessons in life. A short 95-minute flight by Silk Air to Siem Reap will bring you much richness in appreciating cultures, arts, history, legends, ups and downs of a once great civilisation, untold cruelty and human selfishness, etc.

Siem Reap was once the largest city in ancient Asia, with more than one million people. They enjoyed enormous wealth with a rich culture blended inextricably between two major world religions—Buddhism and Hinduism—with a touch of animism. Today, with only about one hundred thousand residents, it is one of the poorest places on earth. With high unemployment, the average salary is less than US$50 a month. The "city" has literally no proper road (mainly mud tracks, which flood frequently), hospital or other infrastructure. Most people are living in wooden houses, in very backward conditions. Its recent war-torn history and political turmoil are still painfully marked by little school-less children hawking souvenirs at temples and beggars with amputated arms or legs innocently but ruthlessly maimed by military mines.

What has happened to this once-upon-a-time great city? Natural disaster? Exterminating diseases? Political upheavals resulting in massive self-destruction by people of the same brethren? Or is it that all great things must come to an end? Be it a country, a company, an organisation or for that matter a person, can we ever sustain or ensure success forever or avoid catastrophic failure befalling upon us without any forewarnings? I won't go into those philosophical reflections in this email. Maybe next time.

Angkor Wat is the largest religious monument built by mankind (larger and grander than the pyramids) and acclaimed as one of the wonders of the world. It is a once-in-a-life-time "must-see pilgrimage" for many Americans and Europeans (surprisingly not quite so for Asians). Two visual impacts struck me very hard.

First, the complexity, ingenuity and scale of the temple's architecture—and wow!—the exquisite beauty of sandstone carvings both on the walls and as standalone figurines. Their extremely fine and intricate craftsmanship could only be exceeded by their rich cultures, legends and religious stories. They creatively symbolise history; tell the story of their wars, their gods and their demons; and boast of their rich, exotic lives. Their bizarre details are mind-boggling. It was captivating and intoxicating for me to watch and admire these ancient artistic creations. How can they create such masterpieces a thousand years ago without CAD-CAM and precision engineering technology?

But there was also other rampant workmanship that delivered to me another form of visual shock—initially with anger and later with sadness. Many of these figurine carvings have been mindlessly "amputated" in various ways by temple raiders or thieves who sell them to the antique market for a tidy sum. Many are irrevocably destroyed with their heads, arms or legs mercilessly cut off, evidently by "cold" electric saws. It is reckless, sinful and indeed criminal to "rape" these world treasures and profiteer by selling them to selfish art collectors. Art collectors must be blamed as they create this market irresponsibly.

As I was touching these great ancient works of art I, too, momentarily relished the dream of owning one small piece of such rare treasure to grace my home or office. "If only I could own just one small piece of such a masterpiece!" I whispered quietly to myself whilst gently stroking the renowned *Churning of the Sea of Milk"*, which was believed to have spurted the nectar of immortality. I quickly came to my senses and reminded myself that I should never succumb to such a sinful temptation just because many have committed such heinous crimes. Several simple questions about morality quickly erased the temptations:

"Why can't we share our precious joy with many, many more generations of people from all over the world by letting these national treasures remain forever in their motherland? It is, after all, their rightful place."

"Can we ever own any earthly things forever in any case? We can't bring them to our grave!"

Key question: "Do we have to own it to love it?"

I know there are many rich and/or powerful people who have "raped" Angkor Wat and taken many ancient art pieces from China, India and other ancient civilisations. They abuse their wealth and/or power to "acquire" such treasures that rightly belong to the people of the country, if not the world! If they asked themselves these soul-searching questions, then they may have the answers to other more important questions in their lives!

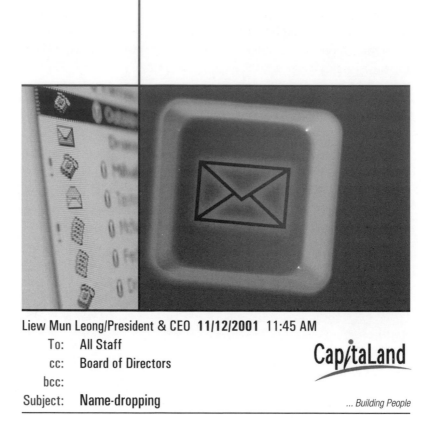

Cap/taLand

... Building People

D uring the last few weeks, our condominium sales have been happily moving quickly again. Both Tanamera Crest and The Levelz are doing very brisk sales. At Tanamera Crest, buyers were queuing up at 5pm one evening for the next day's sale to secure their choice home. We gave them queue numbers and requested that they come back the following morning. The Levelz also experienced the same frenzied response.

This return of good news after the dismal long haul of almost zero sales is, of course, more than welcomed. However, this is accompanied by the return of the most familiar market behaviour—name-dropping to our sales staff. "We know your president or so-and-so, can we get more discount? Can we reserve that unit until we speak to your boss? Can we get this or that extra, so-and-so will agree if we talk to him..."

I got calls over the past weekends from colleagues, telling me about such "harassment". This morning, I had a breakfast meeting with some staff (a small reward for staff who contributed ideas) and name-dropping was brought up again. Steven Foo[1] reminded me that I had previously advised staff during the Pidemco Land days (1998) on how to handle name-dropping and he suggested that I circulate my past email to all CapitaLand staff since the ex-DBS Land staff would not have read it before. Here is how it goes:

"Name-dropping is a communication skill used to influence or exert one's position by associating oneself with important personalities or organisations. You may not realise that this subtle method of influencing behaviour is being used by others on you in everyday life and it has been going on for a long time. You may recall that even as a young kid, someone may utter to you, 'I will tell your mother or father' to try to guide your behaviour in a certain way.

"Though name-dropping may have originated at home, it has been perfected to an art form that is well-practised in the business world and workplace. During discussions, the names of your bosses, president or some political personalities may be mentioned, sometimes blatantly whilst other times more subtly. The hidden game is to influence you to agree to their point of view or concede to some request or to compromise by borrowing someone's name to strengthen or enhance their position. We should take this as their normal method of communication and the best way to handle it is to ignore it. However, if name-dropping is persistent, you should inform the company and we will handle it appropriately.

"My advice is that you should never pay attention or yield to name-dropping in your work. Distasteful as the behaviour may be, you need not respond or be agitated by it. Take it as a sign of weakness of the person who drops names, as only weak people need to build up their image or confidence by riding on someone else's name.

"I ignore name-dropping completely as in almost all cases the purported association with the important personalities were usually not true, and even if they were, they are irrelevant."

End Note

1 Steven Foo is Manager, Marketing and Leasing, CapitaLand Commercial Ltd.

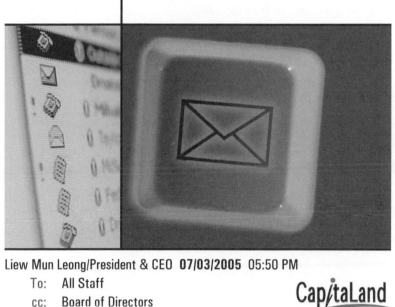

Liew Mun Leong/President & CEO **07/03/2005** 05:50 PM

To: All Staff
cc: Board of Directors
bcc:

Subject: **Corruption's Poison**

Cap/taLand

... Building People

O ur group's strict policy is never to win a deal in a dishonest way—certainly not by bribery. We would rather not do business with anyone anywhere if we have to grease some hands to win a deal. A strong sense of integrity is a cornerstone of our reputation here and abroad. That is fundamental!

What about corporate social responsibility (CSR), the buzz phrase now for corporations in international business? I think the first thing socially responsible multinational companies must do in developing countries—above all others—is not to bribe their way to do business and reject the argument that it is "standard business culture" or "local business practice".

Corruption may be the easy and short-cut answer, but it will finally distort the economy and eventually destroy both the people and the society! There is no point preaching about the environment and human rights issues, etc, if you bribe your way to secure business deals.

Recently, I was interviewed by a senior journalist. After a lengthy discussion on our company's core values and how we conduct business in more than 80 cities, he asked the final pointed question: "You have said that CapitaLand will never give any bribe to secure a deal. What would you say to a shareholder's question that you could have missed out on many good opportunities to make money?"

Instead of replying him directly, I gave him an analogy:

"If someone told you about a restaurant where you can get 'rich and delicious' food at very cheap prices, would you patronise it if you knew that the kitchen is dirty and filthy and you may get food poisoning after that very nice meal?"

The food is fantastic and it is cheap, but you may die dining on that poisonous meal! Maybe you may not die there, but would you risk your stomach, liver or life for the very tasty and cheap food? Most people would say "no way".

I once asked a doctor how safe it is to eat semi-cooked cockles with our favourite char kway teow[1] (炒粿条) in a hawker centre. He likened it to playing Russian roulette—there is only one bullet in the barrel, but that may end your life if it happens to be your unlucky turn!

You may like to live dangerously, but should you expose the company's name and reputation?

Having said that, I think it is not just a question of taking some calculated risks. It is also a matter of our value system. Suffice to say for now that we should be steadfast in our mind, that we should never make money in an immoral way. Whether it is for short-term or long-term gains, we should never move away from our moral conviction in the name of "making money or following local practices"!

By the way, may I remind you that there are three countries I know in the world, namely Singapore, Malaysia and the US, where corruption is a criminal act that has extra-territorial reach. This means that you can be prosecuted in any of these three countries if you are guilty of corruption charges elsewhere in the world, i.e. you can be prosecuted in both the country where the offence is committed and at home for the same offence!

Anyone for semi-cooked cockles in our char kway teow or laksa[2] (叻沙) now?

End Notes

1 Char kway teow, literally "fried flat noodles" in the Hokkien dialect. It is a popular noodle dish in Malaysia and Singapore.
2 Laksa is a popular spicy noodle soup from Peranakan culture, which is a merger of Chinese and Malay elements found in Malaysia and Singapore.

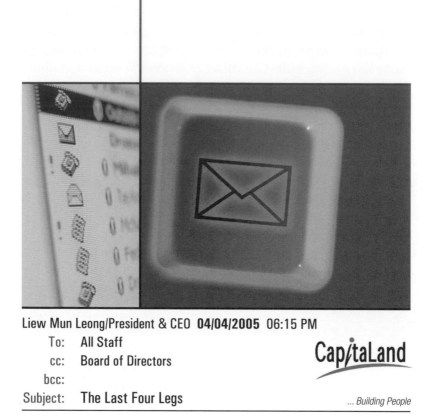

Liew Mun Leong/President & CEO **04/04/2005** 06:15 PM

To: All Staff

cc: Board of Directors

bcc:

Subject: **The Last Four Legs**

Cap/taLand

... Building People

R ecently, I discussed with our hospitality colleagues the importance of maintaining high-quality services for the whole value chain for ALL guests, at ALL times, in ALL places, and under ALL circumstances. It is not good enough to have high-quality services at certain times, then fall into lapses of poor services.

The key word is CONSISTENCY—always providing the same standard of high-quality services.

Personally, I often experience very high-quality service from our hospitality arms. I have also frequently received praise for their good performance from other guests. We are very proud of such compliments. However, there are occasional lapses in services that I and others have encountered. We must maintain consistency.

In my former job as CEO of SISIR (Singapore Institute of Standards and Industrial Research) and as president of the International Organisation for Standardisation (ISO) many years ago, I was actively promoting the importance of standards and quality as a key management system to improve performance. Today, it is a given that companies must practise this if they are to remain competitive.

Let me give you a recent example of consistent, high-quality service that I pleasantly encountered:

I have been staying at the Island Shangri-La hotel in Hong Kong for my business trips four to five times a year for the last 10 years or more. The rooms are large; it has a wonderfully well-equipped and well-serviced gym; it serves a wide spread for breakfast; and the staff are polite and have never failed me in their service so far, be it fast checking-in or checking-out, servicing the room, one-stop customer call or the concierge service. Last week, my stay there gave me again another positive impression.

On Saturday I rang housekeeping for laundry service. It was 11:15am, way past the latest 10am collection time set for the same-day service. I could have been charged 50% more for the same-day service, but the housekeeper kindly told me that she would immediately send someone to pick up the laundry and assured me that it would be delivered before 6pm the same day without any surcharge. She sounded nice and understanding!

The laundry was quickly picked up and I was very happy with that "can-do" positive attitude. I know some hotels in the West that don't even offer laundry service on weekends; and many would not hesitate to charge you more when you are way past the collection time.

Some minutes later, she called and said: "Mr Liew, you have left some money in your jacket. Can we come up and return it to you now?" "Sure, thank you very much", I replied.

A few minutes passed by and again she called.

"Mr Liew, your 'do not disturb' sign is on and my girl is waiting outside your door. Can you please open the door and allow her to return the money to you?"

I thanked her again and rushed to open the door. Sure enough, a young housekeeping assistant was at the door and apologetically said, "Sorry sir, this is your HK$480 (about S$100) left in your jacket. Can you please check it and sign the acknowledgement receipt?"

I gladly did and gave her some gratuity as an appreciation for her honesty and effort. Quite frankly, I would never have realised that I had absent-mindedly left the money in my jacket and may never have missed it at all. All the more, I really appreciated this simple, honest act and the attempts to return the money to me.

This episode shows the honesty and integrity of the staff, but more importantly, the organisation's discipline and values that have been inculcated in the employees. The willingness to accept my late laundry without additional charges also demonstrates the friendly attitude and the flexibility of service-oriented employees as opposed to some unthinkingly rule-driven ones whom I have encountered in other organisations. The commitment to a high level of consistency and perseverance in high-quality services is also reflected in their respecting the "do not disturb" sign and courteously dealing with me to return my money.

This, they say, is the "moment of truth", as quality in the service industry will often depend on what is known as the "last four legs" (the customer's and the last service provider's moment of encounter).

My message here is not intended to glorify our competitor or to make our service staff feel inadequate. Sure, we too can cite thousands of examples of excellent service by our colleagues. The objective is to recognise good standards and learn from them. Sure, I know somewhere, someone will also have experienced lapses of services by Shangri-La, but at least for me, and for a long time, it has left a strong impression of its sustainable good quality service.

It is management's important role to create quality management systems like the ISO9000 to check for quality and its consistency, and then to impose the strict discipline to implement them.

Whether it is in our hospitality services, building an apartment or leasing a shopping mall or office space, the basic principle of executing consistent, high-quality services must still be rigorously applied. How else can we call ourselves a world-class company? Really, there is no point in winning accolades and awards if we cannot be consistent in our high-quality services.

Remember, "THE LAST FOUR LEGS"!

Liew Mun Leong/President & CEO **01/07/2007** 07:43 PM

To: All Staff

cc: Board of Directors

bcc:

Subject: **Where does Corporate Social Responsibility Start?**

Cap*i*taLand

... Building People

What is corporate social responsibility, or CSR? Protecting the world's environment and endangered species, counteracting global warming, building green buildings, philanthropy and charity?

Yes, it's all these, but I have some long-held personal perspectives on CSR and corruption. How are they related? What stimulated my interest in linking these subjects?

HOW IT STARTED

I was speaking at the Harvard China Review Forum in Boston held during the Easter holiday this year. In the audience were more than 300 young and bright Chinese MBA students from Harvard and MIT. I spoke about CapitaLand's business in China and showed a couple of slides on our CapitaLand Hope Foundation's programme, which has built two schools for needy children in Yunnan province.

A young, female Chinese student—looking visibly worked up—spoke up on CSR. She praised CapitaLand's CSR effort to build schools to help poor children in China. In comparison, she bluntly asked a panellist, who is the chairman of a Chinese company, what charity or CSR work his company had done for China, as she couldn't think of any. It caused quite a stir and the Harvard professor who was moderating the session apologetically softened the air for the audience. "This is Harvard", he jokingly pronounced.

The Chinese businessman calmly gave a convincing answer about the company having done quite a fair bit of philanthropy work, including his personal donation. The other panel speakers (Americans) quickly chipped in to highlight their corporate social responsibility programmes too.

But is CSR, I thought, only about philanthropy or doing charity work? I voiced the opinion that CSR or philanthropy work is laudable and should be strongly encouraged. However, for a corporation to do business in any society, whether at home or overseas, the fundamental behaviour for being socially responsible must be the adoption of a zero tolerance policy towards corruption—both within and outside the company. If you practise or condone corruption, all other CSR efforts would come to nothing.

CORRUPTION IS ANTI-CSR

To me, business corruption is the most "anti-CSR" thing to do in any society. It is worthless doing all the big and high-profile philanthropy and CSR work if we tolerate corruption in our business, or worse, make it an accepted way of life. Corruption is a vicious disease, and if not curbed, will spread like cancer causing damage to the very core value system of the society. Why pretend to be socially responsible as a corporation if we corrupt the people in the society we do business in? It is artificial and pretentious.

The young Chinese audience demonstrated their agreement with me with loud, spontaneous applause, and I was touched by these young people's civic-mindedness and their care for society's value system. In this fast-moving, globalising world, it is important to remind young people not to go astray with their value systems, particularly when they are early in their careers.

I feel that senior corporate individuals should shoulder some responsibility in guiding their colleagues, especially the younger ones, on the importance of adopting the right value system. It can make or break them in their future.

PERSONAL PERSPECTIVE—THE EVIL OF CORRUPTION

I have worked in the public sector for 22 years (also in international service when I served as president of ISO in Geneva for three years) and for another 15 years in the private sector. I have done business in emerging and advanced countries. I have worked in science and technology sectors, construction and the property industry. I have seen how corruption can grossly distort the market and a country's economy, and how it can destroy people at all levels. I have seen many bright people ruined their own lives, dismissed from their promising careers when they were caught "dirtying their hands". Several ended up in jail and their families broken up when they finally had to face the penalty of their corrupt wrongdoings. Some had inadvertently "sailed" into such dangerous waters when they thought the world owed them a living and chose what they thought was an easy way to get rich fast. But why the rush?

Regretting is too late for them. Once they touch money illegitimately, there is no turning back and they can never erase their crime—the incriminating facts stay with them for life.

I disagree with the commonly held business notion that you have to bribe your way to do business in developing or emerging countries, that that is a necessary evil and there is no viable choice but to join in the misdeed; otherwise, no business can be done. And that being clean in business is being naive.

It has been CapitaLand's policy that corrupting our way into business is strictly prohibited. Bribery is bad business and our firm stance is that we would not do business in any country if that has to be the way. We have been successful with this strict anti-corruption stance, operating in many developing countries for many years. We will continue with such a policy. It can be done.

MANY BETTER LONG-TERM WAYS TO WIN RELATIONSHIPS

There are many ways to develop business relationships, whether with public servants or private businessmen. We can help in government initiatives like building roads, parks, and schools or contributing to the public activities that benefit the society as a whole. We can help our partners in their job by training them, for example, visiting CapitaLand's overseas projects or conducting formal or on-the-job training for them. In this way, we can build a personal relationship and achieve successful partnerships that produce a positive win-win result for everyone. A beneficial personal relationship between two parties need not be based on corruption. It can be a wholesome, healthy one if we get it right from the beginning.

I have warned our staff that we must never put money in each other's hands. Once it starts that way, it will never stop. It is like drug addiction and just as, if not more, detrimental, because it will affect the whole organisation, even the country.

Recently, a CEO of a Hong Kong property company asked me how we made money in China. I told him that we are a quality developer and there is demand for our products in China. We can build homes, shopping malls and offices well, and sell them well, at reasonable prices. We can secure a decent level of profit margin. I added if we can manage corrupt practices within and outside the company, we can be more certain about making reasonable profit margins in real estate in China, or anywhere else. Just stop the "leakage" and you will have the margin. We have successfully done that, and for more than a decade in China.

Let me relate two more incidents that I remember vividly from two senior civil servants in Singapore:

1) Sim Kee Boon was the permanent secretary of communications and chairman of the executive committee for airport development responsible for the development of Changi Airport in the mid '70s. One day, I remember that as a young engineer involved with the airfield construction, we had to admit to him a technical mistake we made in underestimating the sand reclamation work in Changi. We needed more money—tens of millions—to bring the reclamation to the right, higher levels. In trepidation, we explained the errors to him, expecting some bashing from this top civil servant.

Surprisingly, he didn't beat us up! He rationalised that it was a professional engineering error in estimation and in any case, we do need a certain level of sand fills to make the airport work. He judged that there should be no punishment for such an honest technical error. But he seriously warned, "You put one dollar in your pocket, we will go after you". For us, it was a relief and the right lesson learnt.

2) About 20 years ago, I read a letter written by Philip Yeo (who was then permanent secretary of defence) to someone in a company who was suspected of some unaccountable actions. It was a short letter and one curt sentence stays in my memory until today, "It is better to be poor but proud".

The government public servants are well-conditioned to have a high sense of integrity. That is why they carry a premium for honesty when they seek jobs in the private sector, especially in positions that include the responsibility to safeguard money!

I have been regularly reminding our colleagues about our

anti-corruption stance in our quarterly staff communication sessions. You have heard me nagging on this in management training programmes. It is also a regular feature in our orientation programmes for new staff.

I have explained it this way: In this world there are people with money and there are people with no money. There are people with no money, but who have influence or power over money. As corporate people, we mostly fall into the last category. There would certainly be temptation if we are not steadfast in our moral values and discipline. Don't fall into temptation, as the punishment is so severe that it will destroy your life. I have seen so many lives wasted that way.

I may sound like I am nagging or moralising too much, but it is so important that we get our value system and our reputation on the right footing.

As a corporation we must be socially responsible, but we must start by being responsible to ourselves, our family and loved ones, our company and to society at large.

That, I maintain, is the real meaning of corporate social responsibility. I hope to get more people to understand that.

Chapter 7

Building People –
What It Takes

"Destress. Otherwise, you cannot last for too long. Learn to destress!"

I n many ways, I like the leadership of former General Electric boss Jack Welch and his idea of encouraging team players and team spirit. Fostering a team spirit, where people will try to understand one another and help each other in difficult times, is key to success.

In today's strong economic environment, attracting and retaining talented staff is one of the greatest corporate challenges any CEO must face. I'm aware some of our employees can sometimes be offered two or three times their current salary by competitors to join them. Yet, in most cases they decide to stay.

Compensation is of course an important component of keeping employees happy. People still look at their salary, bonuses and in some cases stock options, and they need to see some progress on their salary if they perform well, which is why I favour a strong pay-performance compensation scheme.

But money is not everything. You can also retain employees by offering them a balanced work-life environment.

I've always been a strong proponent of employees' education, development and training, and I believe a company should give all its employees opportunities to further their knowledge if they wish to do so. I see this as an "investment" in the employees and as part of building bonds between the company and its employees. They may not always stay with us, but they will have benefited from the opportunities and continue to think well of the company. It's all about building people, and part of that building process includes helping each of them to become a more well-rounded person.

Employees should always be guided to maintain the core value system of the company. Leaders and managers must practise what they preach to demonstrate the conviction of what is good for the company.

I also put a strong emphasis on a healthy body for a strong mind because staying in good physical shape has helped me keep fighting fit. My nagging advice to my colleagues is that we cannot do anything great if we are not fit or healthy. I know it needs personal discipline to maintain a regular workout regime. If you cannot keep personal discipline, I think, in any case, you cannot do anything great.

And staying healthy is a personal responsibility. No one can help you stay healthy and fit but yourself.

Liew Mun Leong/President & CEO **08/09/2003** 05:10 PM

   To: All Staff

   cc: Board of Directors

   bcc:

Subject: **Have a Genuine Interest in People**

Cap/taLand

... Building People

During Pidemco Land's early days, I created two taglines:

"Building for People to Build People"—Our external tagline about improving people's lives and society through better buildings.

And:

"Building People to Build for People"—Our internal tagline charting our HR mission to help our people with not only core competencies and the right skills sets, but also the right value systems so that we can all build for others. Building human capital will help us enrich our financial balance sheet with far more leverage for the future.

So we care not only about Buildings, but more importantly, we also care about People.

It may be timely now to repeat these two core value statements as many newly recruited staff have joined us in CapitaLand. I have also found out that many, even senior, staff are not aware of these two fundamental driving principles.

But are we really interested in People?

I am somewhat concerned that we are not quite as deep into it as we should be. Some of us are not really interested in People *per se*.

We may be interested in their talent as a resource, but I can detect that not many are sincerely interested in people as individuals. But we can't be just interested in their talent and ignore the fact that talent originates from People. Having People with talent that is not mobilised is of no use to the company.

And besides talent we must also motivate the rest of the workforce, people who may not be "super geniuses" or "stars", but who can learn through hard work, experience and self-discipline, to get the best from their natural self. They too contribute to the welfare of the company.

Whether they are the very highly talented or the backbone of our workforce, we must first be interested in People. It must start before they join us—scout for them, call them in for an early interview, select them carefully but quickly, understand their strengths and weaknesses, find out their motivation for joining us, give them a well-planned orientation, monitor their progress, communicate with them closely and keep in touch with them regularly until they have been phased in comfortably in their new job.

I have often chided our HR colleagues for letting our job applicants wait too long for an interview. It is like the doctor who doesn't attend fast enough to an anxious patient suspected of a sinister illness. To the doctor it may be just one of many patients, but to the patient it is his life. Trying to get a job in today's high unemployment situation poses the same anxiety to any applicant, and if he is not anxious, he is not a good candidate anyway.

And candidates must be interviewed and assessed by the right level of management; I would suggest the highest possible level, I personally interview all executives who are going to work on the 30th floor of Capital Tower.

One more test. Do we really know our colleagues well and what is happening to them? Quite often, we see them more often than their family members do. Is he stressed because of work or other matters? If he is not performing, what is bothering him? Obviously we shouldn't appear to be too nosey, but we could show some concern, particularly when a colleague appears distressed.

Do you really know your colleagues well—their previous jobs, where they studied, their family and other background, etc? It is really interesting—try finding out. We will understand one another better. Of course, don't intrude into their privacy if they want to be left alone.

Whatever happens to our colleagues we must learn to care for them. Someone once sent me an anonymous quotation: "The mark of a man is how he treats a person who can be of no possible use to him." My view is, "The mark of a man is also how he treats a person even after that person has left us".

Liew Mun Leong/President & CEO **22/10/2004** 04:03 PM

To: All Staff

cc: Board of Directors

bcc:

Subject: **Raising Children, Nurturing Talents**

Cap/taLand

... Building People

A few weeks ago, whilst in the US, I visited my daughter in Boston. She had moved there two months earlier to pursue further studies and it was my first visit to see her there. I brought along mooncakes, barbecued pork from Bee Cheng Hiang,[1] soup mixes and other sundries, all packed into a 40kg suitcase. I wouldn't have lugged such weight along in my own travels if they were for my own personal consumption. Somehow, I did not hesitate to carry out such a burdensome errand for my daughter. Like all fathers, I guess ~ill continue to dote on my children, regardless of how old ~are.

~meone laughed at me as a "filial" father, so typical of

a Singaporean father. My reply was, "our children will always be our children". Isn't it true?

On the flight to the US I was reading a book entitled *Authentic Leadership* by Bill George, the CEO of Medtronic Inc. It is an inspiring book on leadership by undoubtedly a corporate chief, and I recommend that our managers read it. Bill writes that the best advice on raising children comes from Khalil Gibran in *The Prophet*:

Your children are not your children.
They are the sons and daughters of Life's longing for itself.
You may give them your love but not your thoughts,
For they have their own thoughts.
You may house their bodies, but not their souls,
For their souls dwell in the house of tomorrow
Which you cannot visit, not even in your dreams.
You may strive to be like them, but seek not to make them like you,
For life goes not backwards, nor tarries with yesterday.

I think this is very good advice for all parents.

Nurturing talent in an organisation, especially a young one, is like raising children. We must "let them go" so that they can find themselves, and learn to define and reach their own limits.

But like flying a kite, we must still guide the flight upwards or at least provide enough anchorage and support for them so they don't overreach their own capabilities. We need to let go and sometimes we need to pull back. Some cannot manage beyond a certain altitude or fight the strong winds that they may unwittingly challenge. The tiny string must stay, for cutting it too soon, or at all, may sometimes cause a premature end to their otherwise bright future.

End Note

1 Bee Cheng Hiang, established in 1933, is a popular chain in Singapore that sells barbecued meat.

Liew Mun Leong/President & CEO **04/07/2005** 03:06 PM

To: All Staff

cc: Board of Directors

bcc:

Subject: **GNP, not just GDP**

Cap/taLand

... Building People

L ast month, on the Friday morning before Father's Day, I sent my son Karl to Changi Airport. He was flying to Shanghai to begin his new career with a multinational company there under the Asian Business Foundation, a government-sponsored programme to expose young Singaporeans to work in China's fast-growing economy.

I waved him away as he made his departure at the immigration counter with a heavy heart. All my three children are now away from home—two are working in Shanghai (my eldest daughter has been there for two years already) and one is doing her postgraduate studies in Boston.

When my wife and I drove back from the airport, I consoled myself with two valuable pieces of advice given to me before; one by Sir Alan Cockshaw, who once said about raising children:

"Give them roots, give them education, and give them wings"

The other piece of advice was from Ho Ching about growing new companies (and I suppose the same can be applied to bringing up children):

"Grow by letting go."

I was then reminded of another sentiment that I experienced about 24 years ago in 1981 when I first visited China on a business tour. I was travelling on a train from Beijing to Tianjin, and as the train was pulling out of the station, it passed by some farms separated by a chain-link fence, behind which several poorly dressed young children were waving at us. Whilst grinning at us, they had a rather pathetic and envious look on their faces. In 1981, China was then only three years into its economic reforms and the signs of poverty were quite prevalent—a far cry from now! I was told that, within two decades, China has elevated 400 million people above the poverty line.

I told my friends travelling with me that many years ago my parents were hopelessly poor, so they had no choice but to emigrate from southern China to Singapore to make a living. I reminded my friends that, if by chance or choice, my parents were not poor and we had not emigrated out of China, we could have been the ones on the other side of that chain-link fence, waving with envy at foreigners.

Now, my son was flying off to Shanghai for a new beginning. Our children now travel overseas not so much because of poverty or unemployment, but because they have to be well-prepared for new growing markets like, ironically, China.

So the world goes in a full circle and China is back as

the fastest-growing economy in the world. The sooner we understand why we need to let our children and young people go so that they too can prepare themselves for the global market, the better. Singapore has only three million people and 660 square kilometres of land. How many apartments do we want to sell? We need to learn to make money outside our comfort zone and to bring wealth home—to think of GNP, gross national product, and not just GDP, gross domestic product.

That is the route we are charting for CapitaLand. Go International.

Liew Mun Leong/President & CEO **27/12/2006** 01:53 PM

To: All Staff

cc: Board of Directors

bcc:

Subject: **CLIMB and Fill Your CUP**

CapitaLand

... Building People

I was in Japan during the festive season. Some of you may not know that Christmas Day is not a public holiday there, but a normal working day. On the morning of Christmas Day, while jogging on a treadmill at a gym in a Fukuoka hotel, I watched an interesting and inspiring CNN programme. I would like to relate it to you as it should give Singaporeans much pride and it provides some meaningful reflection for us at CapitaLand.

The programme was a CNN special edition entitled *"War on Middle Class"*, anchored by Lou Dobbs, a straight-talking host. Strangely, I think the Americans like to call those not doing economically well as "middle class", possibly to avoid the unglamorous stigma attached to the "working class" label. The session was conducted in an old town hall in Buffalo, New York, with a "middle class" audience and invited guest speakers from all over America. Lou ably led the discussion on issues affecting the middle class, and what could be done for them. He took pride in aligning himself with the audience emotionally, revealing that he came from a "working class" family and presumably could share and understand their experiences and predicaments.

The discussion dwelt on unemployment, large corporations losing jobs overseas, trade protection, and small and medium-sized businesses' struggle for survival, globalisation and global competition, lots of complaints on healthcare and insurance, and lastly, education. There were some very startling facts that the programme talked about:

(a) Healthcare problems

There are currently 47 million Americans who don't have health insurance coverage; one in every five children is not covered. If they are sick and if they don't have the means—and medical costs there can be exorbitant—they can't get medical attention for long. One expert concluded that it was the government's responsibility and that unless Congress works on it there would be no plausible solution. They needed political will to solve this country-wide problem, he contended.

(b) Education standards

One education expert, Tom Loveless, spoke passionately about education standards for poor Americans. He works for a non-profit organisation studying school systems in the country. He lamented that American children don't study enough and have fallen behind many other countries. They especially don't like algebra, geometry and mathematics. When prompted which country was more advanced than the US in education, he readily cited Singapore! He pointed out that Singapore has longer school days, a longer school week, longer school year and more homework. He estimated that by the time an American child leaves school, he or she is two years behind a Singapore child!

I am not a pedagogue and I'm not sure longer school days or more homework is better. I know it is a big debate amongst parents and educators here. But I have met young Americans who can't spell and struggle with simple mathematics in everyday life. On the other hand, young Singaporeans have scored well in international mathematics contests and have won top prizes. Our education system must be doing something right. I figured Loveless is right about how advanced our education system is.

CNN's Lou Dobbs pointed out how his schooling had brought him to where he is today; "It is the best investment for our people", he said. This struck a very meaningful chord with me as, on reflection, I also grew up in a poor working-class family and have benefited enormously from the government's investment to educate me—as with many successful "middle class" or heartlanders. If not for the thorough, perhaps tough education I received, where would I be?

But education, training and upgrading must be a life-long process to enable us to compete in this global market. Everyone of us must continuously learn new skills on the job and gain new knowledge to deepen and broaden our capabilities. For example, if you are an architect or a designer, learn not only to directly strengthen your professional skills, but also learn more about other skills such as financial management, legal or other managerial skills sets.

At CapitaLand, we have recently established CLIMB (CapitaLand Institute of Management and Business) to help upgrade you with well-rounded skills. Be serious about it as this is going to be our competitive edge—each and every one of us must be better trained. Properly run, this will be our life-long passport for survival.

Indeed, CLIMB is our vehicle for the CapitaLand Upgrading Programme, abbreviated as CUP. We must fill up our CUP to compete in this highly competitive globalised world. To me, it is not enough to talk about our "dream". You may notice that

I rarely use the words "dream" and "hope". As in the often aspired to "American Dream", if we are not well-educated when young and don't upgrade continuously in our job, we may end up in what looks like a self-created "American Trap": not enough schooling, no jobs, no healthcare and an inability to get out of the poverty trap, and relying only on social security. This is my personal view on life.

During this festive season, I urge you to remember how fortunate you are to be well provided for in education and healthcare and to think seriously about how to CLIMB and fill your CUP!

Liew Mun Leong/President & CEO **26/03/2007** 08:34 PM

  To: All Staff

  cc: Board of Directors

bcc:

Subject: **Managing Talent, Building People**

Cap/taLand

... Building People

T he successful growth of CapitaLand, both financially as well as our rapid and extensive build-up as an international real estate company, has attracted much interest in how we have been managing our people. At recent discussions with the press and TV media, the favourite question posed to me is about how we manage our talent. We have been complimented for being able to attract and retain a rich talent pool with a strong management bench built up in the last six years. How did we do it?

Managing people and talent has been the subject of extensive studies and research. I have not attended any management school (no MBA) or any formal management programme. So I can't expound any sophisticated theory or model on this perennial management preoccupation. But I do understand, from day one as a manager, that whatever I want to do has to be done by people. It is all about your people decision.

And I have a simple attitude. I simply think it is about finding the right people, building them up and really caring for them. Choose the wrong chap, you get the wrong start. If you don't invest in him, he won't grow to serve you well. If he does well and you don't recognise his contributions and compensate him fairly, he will be poached just as you turn your back. It is therefore very important to get our people decisions right. Simple as that.

Below are some of my personal practical perspectives about managing people.

PEOPLE ARE OUR MOST VALUABLE ASSETS – IS THAT TRUE?

The most important asset on our balance sheet is not our landbank on Orchard Road or our most glamorous shopping malls in China. It is our people. Land has no value if we can't do anything to it—it is only soil or dirt. Our buildings will deteriorate if they are not well-managed or enhanced by our people.

It's often said that for a property company to succeed, it is all about "location, location, location" and "timing, timing, timing". To me, really it's all about "people, people, people"! It is, after all, the people who choose the right location and timing. Of course, this means that they are also responsible for the bad decisions on location and timing. So, if you have the wrong people, they may, instead of being "assets", become "liabilities".

MANAGING TALENT, BUILDING PEOPLE

Managing talent is crucial, but it is equally important to "build people" in the whole company. Each and every one of us should be trained and developed to the maximum, to contribute. We must care not only for the talent, but also for the rest of the group who may not be superstars. Everyone in CapitaLand counts, and we must care for them sincerely.

A few years ago my former driver (he has been with me for more than 17 years now) suffered from a vision problem because of his diabetic condition and could not continue to be my driver. He was a dedicated and loyal staffer and he feared that he would lose his job because of his health condition. We redeployed him to be an office worker, delivering mail and running errands. He is now still gainfully employed with us and continues to be a committed worker. He keeps his job and, most importantly, he knows CapitaLand cares for him. We care even when our employees decide to leave us! Who knows, one day they may wish to come back, and we should then be magnanimous enough to take them back, provided of course they have left on amicable terms and have not done anything to harm us. Respect people and respect their decisions, even if that means they want to leave us. If they are leaving for better prospects, I would compliment them and wish them luck. If they intend to join a not-so-reputable employer, I would give them my fair and frank opinion, but the decision is always theirs.

CARE FOR THEM, BE TRUTHFUL AND SINCERE

Do we really care for our people? We must be sincerely interested in their welfare and not just pay lip service. It is not just about how they have served us in their job and how they perform, but how they are growing with us and their general welfare. We must not blindly manage them with rules and regulations so rigidly that we lack the "milk of human kindness". If we depend only on rules and regulations and are not flexible when the situation arises, we don't need managers and leaders. We can't be ruled by "Instruction Manuals" only! Rules are dead, people are alive. Respect the rules, but we must also use our judgement.

Some years ago, one of our senior colleagues from

Australia who was then assisting us in our first real estate investment trust (REIT) project suffered from cancer, and his medical expenses exceeded our maximum liability under insurance as he was classified as contract staff. We were faced with the official option of sending him back to Australia. Instead, we assured his troubled wife that we would cover all his medical costs to see him through. The couple were very grateful and immediately after recovery he insisted on coming back to work on our first REIT. Unfortunately he had a relapse later and couldn't make it.

The late Lien Beng Thong (he was our general manager of corporate services at CapitaLand China Holdings) did very well with us as our first corporate chief in China. When he passed away suddenly, we quickly facilitated all his entitlements so that the family would not face any economic hardship. More importantly, some of us still keep in close touch with his family. These are just some cases of caring for our colleagues with compassion in whatever difficulties they are in. There are many cases in CapitaLand where our people have gone beyond official duties to care for our colleagues. It is all about a very strong sense of *esprit de corps*, team spirit and the sense of all being in one large family, caring for one another.

THE IMPORTANCE OF A SENSE OF SECURITY FOR THE FAMILY

Increasingly, I realise how important it is to generate financial security for our staff. Recently, in my usual "first night" dinner with our overseas staff and their spouses, I detected a steady sense of confidence in all of them. I can only guess that it is the sense of financial security in the family since our employees are well-compensated with good salaries and cash bonuses, as well as potential gains from stock options, that have brought about this air of confidence in them. They are happily bonded to us. Call it the "golden handcuff".

INTRINSIC MOTIVATION; MONEY IS NOT THE ONLY INCENTIVE

Direct financial rewards, which are what management consultants call "extrinsic motivation", may not be the only incentive to attract and retain talent. The "development returns" are more lasting as a retainer. Are we developing our colleagues in their job in CapitaLand? Are we investing in them? Are they a better executive after working with us for some time? Do they enjoy their job challenges? Are they happy with the environment, the job, colleagues and their working relationship with their supervisors? (Bosses please look after your staff!) Are there "push factors" that they can't resolve themselves? If they are offered several times their current salary, what will overcome such large "pull factors"? Job challenges and satisfaction, pride, career development, sense of achievement and loyalty to the company and colleagues are some "counter-pull factors". Do they feel painful at the thought of leaving us? Sometime ago, two young executives left us to join another group and within a few weeks they asked me to allow them to come back.

CORE VALUE SYSTEM, CORPORATE CULTURE

One more very important consideration is the core value system and corporate culture of the group. Have the staff bought into the core values of CapitaLand? We are comfortable with the corporate culture and core values of the company when the values are more or less aligned with our personal values, too. When we jump into another company we will then realise the differences. Value system, bureaucracy, empowerment, trust and hierarchy chains all vary from company to company.

There is, on the other hand, intrinsic motivation that may lead an employee to stay or leave a company, for example, a sense of mission or other social causes. Our corporate social responsibility programmes like the green programme and CapitaLand Hope School are stimulating quite a strong sense of mission and social cause in the hearts of our staff. Don't underestimate these social forces at work. I am heartened to see strong commitment from staff in these two recently introduced initiatives. They know CapitaLand is not only about making money. We do good for others and they are all for it.

MAVERICKS VS. CORPORATE PEOPLE

As a property company we need entrepreneurial people to create opportunities, take risks and do deals. We can't just sit down, collect rent and wait for our buildings to appreciate in value, like antique collectors—no challenge, and young, restless talent will soon abandon us. Talented people, like all other mavericks, are very easy to motivate, but difficult to manage. We can empower and trust them to break the frontier in order to "bring home honey and ham". But we will also need a well-thought-through corporate system to guide them. Hence, we have invested in corporate and organisational people to plan for the future, organise resources and systems for doing business in a co-ordinated way and spot potential missteps way in advance.

We now have high-calibre people in corporate planning, research, HR, development and training, finance, communication, investor relations, risk management and audit. These corporate people are also the best we can find, as they have very strategic and important tasks to perform. Their mistakes may have huge impact throughout the company as they will affect all the business units in the whole group.

On the other hand, mavericks must learn to work with everyone, including the corporate forces that are not there just to check them, but also to support and help them to avoid slips or missteps. In short, we need talent in both the maverick business group as well as in the corporate support group. And both must work together. A maverick who can only make tons of money in his own backyard will face his own limitation in the group. Managing talent requires managing the balance between the mavericks and the corporate forces so that they can harmoniously work together without discouraging either type of talent.

"Building for people to build people" and " Building people to build for people". This is what we are doing to manage talent and to build people!

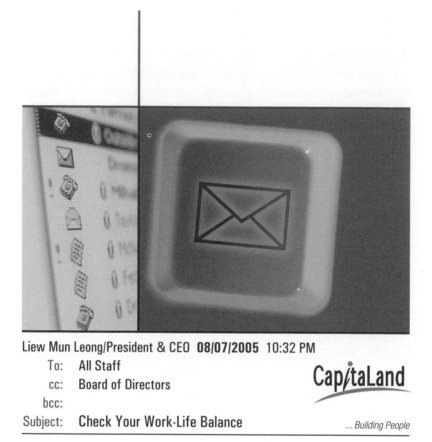

Liew Mun Leong/President & CEO **08/07/2005** 10:32 PM

To: All Staff

cc: Board of Directors

bcc:

Subject: **Check Your Work-Life Balance**

Cap/taLand

... Building People

L ast week, whilst reviewing the performance of our staff, I discovered that quite a few are in poor health. This is quite worrisome. Several colleagues are not well and they are either taking a break from the office, requesting to do lighter jobs or going for early retirement. Perhaps the demands of a challenging job in a rapidly expanding company and managing a family have become overly stressful.

Just two nights ago, I received an email informing me that one of our young and capable colleagues is not in very good shape, probably because he is too stressed answering complaints about his project. I was very worried by this piece of bad news.

I asked myself:

(1) Are we overly ambitious in our business goals? Are our targets or performance indicators too stretched? Are we putting too much stress on our staff with these high-level targets? Are these high targets necessary and reasonable?

(2) Are we really grossly understaffed to the extent that everyone has to do more or even double up?

(3) Are our colleagues pushed to do jobs beyond their abilities—what we call in management "Peter Principle"— people being promoted to their level of incompetence and subsequently being unable to perform in their new, higher or expanded, role.

(4) Is management supportive, sympathetic and caring enough to help struggling colleagues in their work?

(5) What can we, as the employer, do about it?

(6) Is it just normal Singaporean culture to be stressed out, as has been observed by many foreigners? Worse, is it a part of our Singaporean culture to wear stress like a proud badge and assume that people who do not appear to be under stress are not "good executives" or are not working hard enough?

These issues were discussed at the last CEO Council meeting. I have suggested that HR study this subject thoroughly. I have also proposed employing a stress management consultant from Singapore General Hospital or a private health group to assist us in evaluating our staff's stress level and to give talks on how to manage stress and health better. Although we do not have all the answers to the questions above just yet, management is very concerned and will study this subject.

You may find it strange that I am talking about work-induced stress, as some fingers will surely point at me or management as the culprit. I am sure your stress level cannot be very much higher than mine, but I can tell you what I do to destress.

(1) I do an intensive workout every day in the morning; 45 minutes of jogging and some weights, followed by a good bath. I will be in the office charged with energy and enough endorphins to "kill a bull". Physical exercise is surely one very important way to take stress away.

(2) I find good and responsible talent to help run CapitaLand. Delegate and farm some stress to them, but make sure they can carry it and will not collapse under it. Help them grow and they will help me in destressing.

(3) Have a good circle of friends, family members, loved ones or other support group to air your frustrations generated from work. It is healthy to talk about problems and let off steam. Better still, develop a sense of humour! Learn to look at the lighter side of things and laugh at your adversities.

(4) Relax and have a good hobby or recreational activity. I play golf on weekends now, and believe it or not, writing emails to staff (like this one) on Sundays is quite enjoyable and relaxing. Get whatever entertainment you enjoy or just do something other than work. I watch Cantonese movies on DVD, video, etc, before I go to sleep as a form of relaxation and distraction. Watching colourful and swash-buckling martial arts heroes jumping about in complicated Chinese stories is good escapism from the harsh reality of everyday life!

(5) I try to get some solitary moments for private reflection every day. I do that during my morning jogs. I find that

my mind is clearer for the day. I think it is also healthy to learn to do nothing sometimes!

(6) I give myself plenty of time and space. I leave early for the airport and do not rush to the gate at the last minute. Air travel is stressful enough and there is no need to add more stress to it. Likewise, I go to meetings early in case there is an unexpected traffic jam. Even if you are caught in a traffic jam, there is no point in getting stressed out when you can't control the situation. That is something we can learn from the Thais, who seem to have mastered the art of coping with traffic jams in Bangkok! Prepare for your meetings ahead of time. Last-minute reading is no fun.

(7) Finally, I enjoy my job. If you don't enjoy your job it is difficult to work long hours and stay committed to producing good work. Your job is so much a part of your life that it shapes you and makes you what you are. If you intensely dislike doing what you are doing, and in this regard, you need to be honest with yourself, then it is no wonder that getting to work everyday is a chore and every assignment will add to your unhappiness and stress. Then, obviously, you are not in the right place. Need I say more?

Whatever your method to destress is, please remember that your health is your personal responsibility and no one in this world can really manage your stress level or any other health conditions for you. You are the best person to know your own capabilities, limitations and your priorities in life (I know some of you don't). Somehow, each one of us must find that balance in our lives. I believe that what you do must challenge you, otherwise you are not developing or improving.

We are not here to run a country club. We have corporate objectives and missions to fulfil for our shareholders. Having said that, we are not robots either and we certainly do not want employees to turn into work machines. It is very important for every one of you to find that right balance, and I am sure you can then have fun and enjoy your work in CapitaLand, as I do.

So learn to relax during weekends and get ready for a fresh week with an able and strong body and mind for more fun and excitement when you get to work.

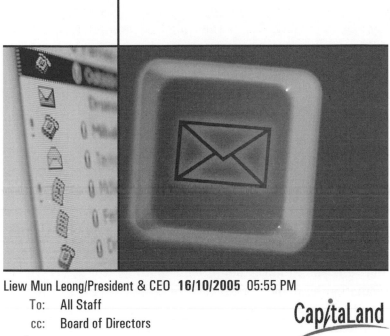

Liew Mun Leong/President & CEO **16/10/2005** 05:55 PM

To: All Staff

cc: Board of Directors

bcc:

Subject: **Find that Balance!**

Cap/taLand

... Building People

R ecently, I visited a senior colleague who was recuperating at home from a minor heart problem. He wrote to thank me for all our well wishes and complimented me as the perfect model of working hard and still maintaining a sense of balance. I replied to him with some advice on what I do to maintain that balance. Below is part of my email to him:

I just thought about giving you a call but your email preceded that. My own recipe is to work very hard, but to relax well and to be able to destress quickly. My daily routine tells it all. I spend three private hours by myself first thing in the morning, every morning unless I am flying somewhere. I jog and workout on the machines. I then have a cold bath and a quick breakfast and set off to the office, refreshed to start the day.

From 6am, when I wake up, to 9am when I step into my office I have already enjoyed the first and best three hours of my day, every day. That is the time I am absolutely alone, not talking to anyone and in complete privacy. It is the best time to reflect on what is happening or going to happen. I reserve that time to think through the most difficult problems I may have on hand. It is my most imaginative time, very productive and enjoyable! This is my "third place", the first being my home, the second being the office. Try it.

Next, I enjoy my work—frankly, if we are not enjoying our work we can never work hard—and will never do well. We must make changes to have more fun in our work. Find out what motivates us, what we want in life (besides more money) and why. If not, quit and do something else. We only have one life.

Right now our group provides lots of opportunities and fun. The group is doing well and has won a very good reputation here and abroad. The real estate market in Asia is growing; we now have a strong balance sheet and we have developed a unique real estate value chain proposition to win in the market. World-class companies are talking to us about possible partnerships. We have already established strong partnership networks in many countries, and we have talented and dedicated people working with us, though I still think we should recruit more.

I am having lots of fun in my work—I've never had it harder or better in my life—and I really wish you all will do the same. What's more, we are all rewarded well. Many of our colleagues have recently become millionaires with their stock option gains, and there should be many more to come as our prospects improve. Morale is at an all-time high not because of stock option gains alone but because we have won a strong reputation for ourselves—something that many analysts and investors did not believe we could do five years ago when we started CapitaLand. Now even the most pessimistic of those analysts and journalists are writing in our favour.

What do I do other than jogging and workout? I do some community work, something that is beyond thinking about my own "rice bowl".

From 1978 till the late '80s I did some work in community centres and I found it mentally rewarding. I enjoyed learning to work with the community to solve its problems. It is a good distraction and we can always learn something from it. I've chaired the Board of Governors of Temasek Polytechnic for seven years now and I have fun working with 16- and 17-year-old students, trying to understand what they want and their aspirations. It makes you young, thinking along with them!

Recently, I was asked to chair the Civil Aviation Authority of Singapore—Changi Airport, which I helped build 30 years ago. I am very proud that Changi Airport has gone on to be rated as the best airport in the world for many years. This chairmanship position will mean more work for me, but will also require different thinking skills to handle different types of challenges. I find that it enriches my mental faculties and my brain needs different types of exercise.

I've also served on the Council of Corporate Disclosure and Governance for three years now, making a nuisance of myself there trying to understand how regulators and accountants think! It's a lot of work, but quite a break from my normal real estate business! Yes, some distraction is good, but of course there must be balance—we should know who is feeding us and our family!

Yes, I also have a hobby and it is golf! It takes time, but it is actually very relaxing. There can be many lessons to learn from the sport that can relate to management practice and life in general. Golf completely distracts you from work when you are concentrating, trying to hit a ball. If I do not focus, I can hit like a cow and make a fool of myself. Hit a good one and it will make my day. But mind you, it is very addictive and time-consuming; you've got to plan it out with your family. Nine holes in the late afternoon is my convenient slot.

My next joy is reading. There is so much to read, not just on our work, but also to get to know the world at large. I observe with regret that our young people don't read enough. At job interviews, very few candidates have read enough to impress me. The best time for me to read is when I'm on a flight; I bought three books yesterday and I just can't wait to dig into them—alas, I must wait for the next flight when I can find enough time to read them.

For a really relaxing pastime I watch an hour of a Cantonese movie on DVD every evening just before I go to bed. Be it martial arts, Chinese legends or some modern-life sob stories, they put my mind to rest. No thinking needed, just a dose of fantasy to end the day. It is my daily "escapism".

Lastly, my final tip is to meet up with friends, especially old ones who have no business relationship with you. Have a drink and a nice chat once in a while. It is worth spending time with friends to give you a perspective of how others are living out their lives, so that you don't lose touch. We need friends, and, I tell you, more so when we grow older.

Just thought I'd share with you how I strike the balance between the hard demands of my work and taking it easy. The group is doing well and growing fast and we need each and every one of us to be in the best health, both mentally and physically and in good work-life balance, to bring it forward. Take good care!

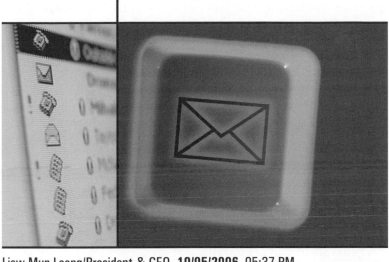

Liew Mun Leong/President & CEO **10/05/2006** 05:37 PM

To: All Staff

cc: Board of Directors

bcc:

Subject: **Your Health is Your Personal Responsibility**

Cap/taLand

... Building People

L ast year, I shared with you my concerns on the demands of a challenging job on our health in a rapidly expanding company like ours. I stressed the importance of striking a balance between our lives, our family, our health and our job.

I then asked HR to work out a comprehensive plan to find out the state of health of all employees and to provide help and support to address any health issues.

Together with Raffles Medical Group, we are launching a "Total Well-Being Programme", which incorporates both physical and mental well-being. This is a holistic wellness programme, which consists of a self-assessment to bring about awareness of your lifestyle and your state of health, as well as a physical health screening. Various programmes and support will be made available to you.

An invitation to a communication session on this programme has already been sent out. The Total Well-Being Programme commences with a series of employee communication sessions to be conducted by doctors from Raffles Medical Group to give you a comprehensive overview of the programme, what it means to you and how you can make use of it.

We have made a lot of effort devising this programme and I strongly encourage you to attend and participate in the communication session and in the programme.

As I have said before, your health is your personal responsibility. Please make good use of this programme and take the first step to becoming healthier.

Take care and keep well!

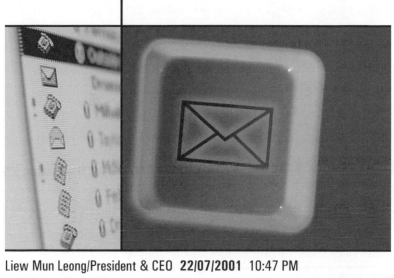

Liew Mun Leong/President & CEO **22/07/2001** 10:47 PM

    To: All Staff
    cc: Board of Directors
    bcc:
Subject: **There are No Fat CapitaLand Executives**

Cap/taLand

... Building People

I wish to instil a "keep fighting fit" corporate culture in CapitaLand. Here is my long pitch again.

American executives are "bloody" fit. When I travel in Asia and Europe, the hotel gym ordinarily opens at between 8am and 8:30am, and some, unreasonably, open even later on weekends. Most are poorly patronised. Last week, I used the hotel gyms in several US cities and I saw a different usage pattern. They are busy from 6am onwards until sometimes as late as 11pm.

And the size! I thought the Americans only have large trading floors—the largest I have seen was 120,000 sq ft (11,148 sq m) (compared to our largest at 35,000 sq ft) and could house

1,000 traders. My goodness, they also build large gyms—the one in New York that I went to was 150,000 sq ft over six floors. By 6:30am, it was almost all filled by sweating souls—both young and old and of all shapes and sizes. My American hosts who travelled with me were also active gym users. The two of them are in their early 50s and are energetic. They met me every morning before breakfast at the gym by 6:30am. So far, none of my business associates in Asia or Europe has been as crazy about fitness.

If we are not fighting fit, how can we cope with this everyday high-speed life? The best way to destress is through an active workout. Good for your mind and body. I have been jogging for many years. When I took over Pidemco Land in 1996, I increased my efforts to 30 minutes (from 20 minutes) three to four times a week.

When the great idea of the merger came, stress built up, but that was no problem, I just stepped up the workout programme. Now I jog for 45 minutes, seven days a week—unless I'm ill or I'm flying early in the morning. It is a great regime and I have never felt fitter! I just had my medical checkup and passed every test. The merger did me good!

I will tell you how I manage this long jogging routine—I start to do my daily "thinking" during the 45-minute workout. I automatically feel a sense of detachment between my body and my brain. When I put on my thinking cap, I don't feel tired or bored. It is the best time to do some uninterrupted, serious reflection. Some call it the third wind. Maybe we can think much more clearly because more oxygen rushes to our head. So I have developed the habit of reserving a difficult problem for the morning jog, to think it through. My best ideas, clever solutions, great shakes and thinking will come through then.

Several recommendations here:

(i) Do your workout in the morning. Your metabolism is faster and your body burns more calories. You will feel light, healthy and a sense of well-being first thing in the morning. It is like morning morphine for me.

(ii) Eat well and eat healthily. As the doctor says, "you are what you eat". Take care not only about the quantity, but also the quality and how the food is prepared. One can of soft drink has 100 to 120 calories—equivalent to six teaspoons of sugar! Stop taking deep fried food and avoid (no need to completely give up) oily fried things like char kway teow (炒粿条). Once in a while let go, indulge yourself, but again, take control, please.

(iii) Keep a scale and weigh yourself every day. It does wonders when you are reminded daily. Calculate your BMI (body mass index = weight divided by the square of your height) and stay within a range of not more than 25. You can't control or manage it if you don't measure it. This is based on what is called metrology in engineering, the science of measurement.

(iv) Think of the consequences if you are not healthy—get sick easily and have to go "upstairs".[1] What is the consequence to you, your family and your loved ones? Recently, over a casual talk after dinner, I encouraged a good friend to control his diet and take up jogging to reduce his belly. I told him bluntly, "You must be responsible to your family. Who will look after them if you go?" He has three lovely young children, the last one barely one year old. He is a very loving father and that got to him. He is now jogging regularly, controls his diet and even stopped smoking!

(v) An easy motivation for all—exercise will enhance your looks and give you a better figure. Think about all the "fierce" clothes you can wear if you lose a few kilograms.

But really, if you exercise—I don't care if you jog, walk, swim, play tennis or even dance (incidentally Jennie Chua told me she regularly dances three hours)—you will be a better-looking person. If you look good, feel good, you will do "good". You will enjoy life more—take it from me.

Is this too much nagging on a personal subject? My last message at the management retreat was, "There is no fat executive in CapitaLand".

So get out, you lazy bones, and get going. It is all about discipline and then habit. It is going to be our corporate culture to be fit.

Have fun doing it!

End Note

1 "Going upstairs" here is a colloquial way of saying "going to heaven" or "to die".

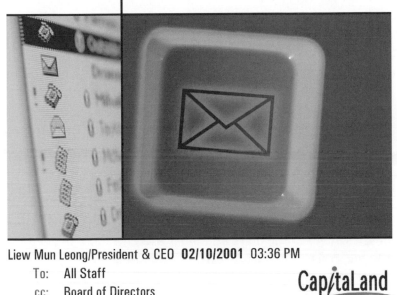

Liew Mun Leong/President & CEO **02/10/2001** 03:36 PM

To: All Staff

cc: Board of Directors

bcc:

Subject: **Sentosa Sunday**

Cap/taLand

... Building People

T he Walk-A-Jog at Sentosa on Saturday morning was a great success. Despite the heavy rain in the morning, almost 500 people turned up at 8:30am. It was more than a workout.

The rain did not deter the spirit of our colleagues who came with their families. Several were even in their rain coats. What inspired me most was Ng Theng Kioh from PREMAS who brought along his wife and father. His father is 85 years old and he completed the 5.2 km journey! Seemed no sweat for this elderly gentleman. Are you inspired to keep fit?

Another senior executive, Chng Chet Siew[1] from Raffles Holdings, came with her husband. He is currently on an exercise regime and has lost more than 10 kilograms over the last few months. His waistline has reduced from 36 inches to 33 inches. Another inspiration!

I met a senior member of staff who joined PREMAS in August. He used to be the chief engineer in ANA Hotel[2], which now, coincidentally, belongs to CapitaLand Residential. I introduced him to Tham Kui Seng, who now knows who to go to if ANA Hotel has technical trouble.

At this social event we could interact with people of all ages and ranks from all over the group. I "ran into" several staff and updated myself with what's going on with them. It was a great chance to chat with and get to know them better. During the jog, I was paced all the way by a young executive, Thomas Kong from CapitaLand Residential. He was born in 1972—two years after I had graduated and started my first job!

My final verdict—I think 80% of the group is not quite physically up to the mark and must exercise more to keep up. We must keep fit during this international crisis period to destress. I encourage all staff to keep up with their physical fitness—jogging, gym, walking, games, etc—whatever it takes to keep you in shape both physically and mentally. We need to keep ourselves sane. Take it from me—it is very enjoyable once you cultivate the habit and discipline. For the next jogging session, do bring along your family to join us.

My thanks to the organising committee for organising this Walk-A-Jog session so successfully and economically.

End Notes

1 Chng Chet Siew is now head of Group Leasing in CapitaLand Retail Limited.
2 ANA Hotel was officially opened in January 1979 as Century Park Sheraton Singapore. It was renamed ANA Hotel Singapore in September 1990. The hotel and its site were acquired by the then-DBS Land in August 1999. DBS Land subsequently merged with Pidemco Land to form CapitaLand Group. The site has been re-zoned for residential use.

Liew Mun Leong/President & CEO **18/03/2002** 06:06 PM

To: All Staff

cc: Board of Directors

bcc:

Subject: **A Broken Leg Reminder**

Cap/taLand

... Building People

I often speak about personal fitness and the importance of building a strong body for a strong sense of well being. A rigorous morning workout will do the job. Then every morning you can walk into the office charging like a "bull".

I am a firm believer and practitioner of that routine. But today, I felt downright miserable.

Yesterday, I fell and injured my right leg and suffered an excruciatingly painful helical (curved) crack in my fibula bone. This leg is now cast in plaster and I have to use crutches, which, I've discovered, requires strong hand muscles and skill to move my body around. More difficult is overcoming the embarrassment of strange stares in public places like lobbies where elevators seem to take ages to arrive.

Just one day into this new experience, I am already frustrated like hell with my immobility. When I see people running around, I envy their ease of movement. Now I can appreciate an able body much more!

You never appreciate the value of an able body until you are at risk of not having one. I'm not able to travel and had to postpone four scheduled trips over the next six weeks. No more gym, golf, shopping or hopping around restaurants or hawker centres. Luckily, we have the China Club just upstairs!

Take it from me—a healthy and able body is worth a lot, and you don't realise how much it means until you lose it, even for one day! So keep up your fitness regimes.

Ironically, Raffles Hospital was just officially opened by DPM Lee[1] on Saturday morning and I was there representing CapitaLand as half owner of the hospital. Almost exactly 24 hours later, I was wheeled in as a patient. Loo Choon Yong, the chairman of Raffles Hospital, jokingly said that I was a good shareholder supporting the hospital!

End Note

1 The then Deputy Prime Minister Lee Hsien Loong is now the Prime Minister of Singapore.

Chapter 8

Nurturing Our Soul

"Building for People to Build People;
Building People to Build for People."

I have not always embraced the idea of corporate social responsibility (CSR). When this term was coined a few years ago, I first thought there was little point for big multinationals to wear their CSR on their sleeves in Asia when some of them continued to "corrupt" countries by handing out kickbacks to win business. We will walk away from any market if participating in it necessarily means we have to bribe. That is our policy.

Fighting corruption is the first step to good CSR. That said, a multinational corporation like CapitaLand does have increased responsibility to the community, and while it is harder to justify a focus on charitable causes to shareholders, especially in hard times, I've always believed in the motto, "doing well, while doing good". We can do good business in a good way.

In the spirit of our credo "Building for People to Build People; Building People to Build for People", CapitaLand believes in giving back to society and the communities in which it operates. The development of a society cannot be divorced from the development of the people, and the development of a company cannot be divorced from that of its employees.

While we had in the past given to charitable causes on an ad-hoc basis, we decided in 2005 to formalise this commitment, and set up the CapitaLand Hope Foundation to focus our efforts on giving back to the communities where we operate. CapitaLand Hope Foundation was formed after we successfully built facilities for two schools in Yunnan for very poor children. The experiences were very inspiring and it touched our soul on what we can do to help poor young children build their future.

The foundation is also an extension of our aspiration to be a lasting company that creates value for its stakeholders, including the community at large. It is an avenue for us to rally greater staff participation in community activities for the needy and underprivileged. CapitaLand Hope Foundation focuses only on helping needy and underprivileged children in three main areas—building shelter, health and education. Our other corporate social responsibility activities will centre around environmental consciousness through the building of green buildings, cultural exchange and provision of scholarships to deserving tertiary students.

The company will raise funds through charity events led by its employees, and aims to donate up to half a percent of its net profit every year into the foundation. It should be able to receive a few million dollars every year unless we do badly, which we won't!

I believe this foundation allows all the various efforts to be more systematic and co-ordinated, while ensuring transparency and accountability to the company's shareholders. We are also more focused on helping young children—our very important future.

In the end, it isn't only about earning the goodwill of the communities in which the company operates, but also about doing good for the soul.

Liew Mun Leong/President & CEO **20/04/2005** 06:25 PM

To: All Staff

cc: Board of Directors

bcc:

Subject: **Building People to Build People**

Cap/taLand

... Building People

I would like to tell you about some heart-warming initiatives that our colleagues in China have been engaged in to help poor children in China's Yunnan province.

Several years ago, the Chinese authorities initiated the Project Hope[1] programme to promote education in China's rural, poverty-stricken areas. Last year, at the official opening of Raffles City Shanghai, our colleagues successfully raised RMB770,000 (about US$93,000) by putting charity donation boxes in our shopping centre as well as in our property sales showrooms.

Shanghai city is given the role to look after the welfare of the poorer Yunnan province. We therefore decided that the funds raised at the Raffles City Shanghai launch be donated to assist in improving the facilities of the schools in Yunnan. Two schools in two very remote and rural villages in Yunnan, somewhere near the Myanmar border, were selected by Shanghai officials, and the donations were used for building new school facilities. Each school received RMB300,000 from the funds collected.

Last week, a group of us had the privilege of attending the ceremonies to unveil the two buildings. The first site was a dormitory site in the hilly Cuiyun District, which is an hour's drive on largely unpaved and rocky mountainous roads from a small city called Simao where we had stayed overnight after a whole day of flying from Shanghai to Kunming, the capital of Yunnan. The journey was arduous, but it proved to be very rewarding when we arrived at the foot of the mountain slope to walk to this CapitaLand Hope School in Cuiyun District.

The mountain track towards the school was lined with about 300 children from the elementary level, cheering loudly "Welcome! Welcome!" Our donations have been used to construct a dormitory block for boarding children. In the past, the dropout rate from the school was high because the children had to walk between 8 km and 12 km on mountain tracks, across rivers and through patches of jungle, to reach the school. With the completion of this dormitory, the students can now reside in the dormitory block from Mondays to Fridays and return home to their parents on Saturdays and Sundays. In addition, the students were each given a very nice, colourful school bag. We handed them out one by one to the children and you could see the glee in their eyes. Even though the bags cost only about RMB30 each, they were very happy with them. I think it must be the biggest present they had received in their lives, considering their household income per month averages RMB200.

In my speech, I told them that whilst I was walking up the slope to the school, I had recollections of myself at their age, some 50 years ago, in Singapore. I reminisced that back then, Singapore was similarly impoverished. Many of us may not remember or know about the poor rural areas in the then undeveloped areas of Toa Payoh, Ang Mo Kio, Kim Keat, Jurong and Havelock Road, places where most of us were still staying in kampongs[2] and villages with unpaved roads, some even without electricity and with very few decent schools. I encouraged the students to study hard, build good careers, be filial to their parents and one day they may be like us, going to other places to help other less-privileged children. The villagers and government officials were visibly pleased with such encouragement. Funny, they called me "Liao ye ye" (廖爷爷 – Grandpa Liew!); I still haven't gotten used to accepting that term of respect yet!

The next day, we drove to a place called Lancang County. Again, some five to six hours' drive across some dusty mountain tracks in our Land Rover. The CapitaLand Hope School in Lancang County also offers elementary education to around 250 students. This is the only elementary school in the county, which is home to the Hani minority tribe. The existing school is dilapidated, and has leaks and broken window panes. The funds raised had been used to build a new classroom block—no frills, just a decent concrete and brick structure. Here again, the same degree of warmth and enthusiasm greeted us, although the children were clearly even more poverty stricken. The girls have to sleep on planks on muddy clay floors. They only have old and torn blankets to keep themselves warm. I was told they had to huddle together to keep warm when the weather gets too cold. I know as a matter of fact that it does get quite cold there because the temperature dropped to about 10 degrees Celsius the night I was there, and it was already April! Our children should see and experience this!

Funny, in this school, the students addressed me as "Liao shu shu" (廖叔叔 – Uncle Liew) and I jokingly told them how happy I was to be one generation younger after one day of travel.

These journeys to participate in a programme for poor children in China have been a real eye-opener for us. China is not just about Shanghai, Beijing or Guangzhou. It is good to remember that there are still 800 million people who live in poor, rural areas. Being aware of the existence of minority races (there are 56 different minority races in China) and the standard of living that they have is important for us to keep the perspective of what China is all about. These people may not contribute directly to our bottom line, but certainly our motto "Building for people to build people" cannot be more heartfelt than on such occasions, when we build homes and schools for the needy, and not for the purpose of making a profit!

I sincerely hope that in building for people, we are also able to build our people to have values that go beyond simply achieving hard business targets and profits. We should build a company that our people can be proud of. Our people should feel good about themselves and feel proud of the company that they work for and the values that the company stands for!

I told Ming Yan that as we do business in China, we should play our part in contributing to its community in the manner that we do best, build useful structures or buildings for them! Similarly, we should also adopt this approach to all other countries where we have our operations and businesses.

I came back from this trip reflecting on how fortunate we are that our children can enjoy modern buildings for homes, schools, shopping malls, etc, and how fast we have moved in the last 50 years to where we are today. We must remind ourselves that if we do not maintain our momentum of progress, we may actually go backwards and deteriorate. We should be mindful that China was once, and for a long time, one of the most powerful and wealthy countries in the world!

Notwithstanding the hardships of that journey, we really enjoyed the trip tremendously—learning about the people and their lives. We feel really good about what we have done. They have made me the honorary principal of the two schools and I told them that I will go back to visit them in a year or two to see how they have fared.

End Notes

1 CapitaLand is a strong supporter of Project Hope in China, an initiative by the Chinese government to help children in poor rural areas receive elementary education. In conjunction with the official opening of Raffles City Shanghai, CapitaLand pooled contributions from staff, mall shoppers and homebuyers. The funds were used to sponsor the construction of premises for two CapitaLand Hope Schools in Yunnan's remote areas of Cuiyun and Lancang in 2005, which were later visited by Liew Mun Leong, who also launched computer resource rooms in both schools.
2 Kampong is "village" in Malay.

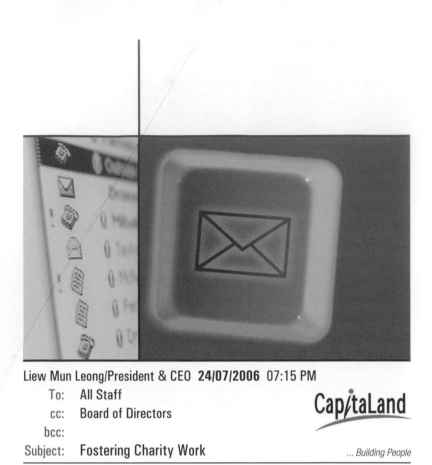

Liew Mun Leong/President & CEO **24/07/2006** 07:15 PM

To: All Staff

cc: Board of Directors

bcc:

Subject: **Fostering Charity Work**

Cap/taLand

... Building People

Yesterday I spent the whole day—first at home, then in the office—digging up "old things" to sell at the Charity Bazaar that CapitaLand is organising this coming Sunday. It was a labourious day for me, but at the end of it I felt very good. Our Charity Bazaar is organised in association with the Ministry of Community Development, Youth and Sports and will benefit the students of the Canossaville Children's Home.

I managed to gather quite a big pile of "old things" to sell for charity, though some of them may bring back strange memories of how and why I acquired or bought them in the first place. Some were gifts and I hope I will be pardoned for putting these gifts up for sale for charity. Anyhow, most, if not all, haven't been used in years. I shall not miss them and I think my friends or loved ones who gave me those gifts wouldn't mind me donating them to charity.

I achieved the following outcomes:

(1) I cleared my office and home of things I don't need or have not used for years! Why keep them to clutter my surroundings?

(2) Instead of them lying idle and occupying space, I could sell them for a price that will then be donated for a good cause.

I encourage you to try to do what I did—get rid of all unwanted things lying idle, at home or in the office, and in the process do some good for charity. You will enjoy this simple physical exercise. Believe me, doing that also clears your cluttered mind! You now have until Thursday, or at the latest Friday, to do this. Act now! Of course, this is a little difficult for our overseas colleagues to do so this time round, but they may organise a similar event in their host country.

As a commitment of our company to this event, I am pleased to share that CapitaLand Hope Foundation will match a dollar for every dollar raised during this project.

Chapter 9

Media Interview 1

The CEO Who Enjoys Being Difficult

This interview was first published in The Sunday Times, *31 October 2004.*

CapitaLand Chief Executive Liew Mun Leong is living proof that bureaucrats can make good businessmen. He wants the property giant to be known as one that drives a hard bargain when it buys services, but also gives its best to customers.

"Former civil servant" is a label that Mr Liew Mun Leong wears with indignant pride.

The civil engineer by training started life developing

military camps and infrastructure for Singapore's Ministry of Defence, then led the construction of Changi Airport.

After 22 years in the civil service, he joined the private sector in 1992, as group managing director and CEO of the then-largest engineering and construction firm, L&M Investments, amid niggling doubts over whether a bureaucrat could cut it as a businessman.

Three-and-a-half years later, he had transformed the company and doubled its share price. Still, the nay saying persisted as he took on his next job as president of Pidemco Land and Singapore Technologies Properties in 1996. In 2000, a merger between Pidemco Land and DBS Land created CapitaLand, Southeast Asia's biggest property player, and he was named CEO, again amid some scepticism.

It has taken more than a decade, but these days, he is finally recognised as an astute businessman and deal-maker who has taken the government-linked property giant global.

CapitaLand now has operations in 78 cities with more than 65% of earnings coming from overseas. In the last four years, it has successfully monetised S$7.6 billion (US$4.37 billion) of assets, despite weak market conditions, and grown revenue by 31%, from $2.9 billion in 2000 to $3.8 billion last year.

The irrepressible 58-year-old lets rip on rebranding CapitaLand, why he only sends A-graders abroad and how he enjoys being difficult.

Q: You are proof that bureaucrats can make good businessmen. But it took a while to convince others. Why do former civil servants get such flak in the market? Are you the exception or the norm?

A: In the civil service, I was always arguing, asking why can't we do this and that and breaking the rules. So that was my preparation for the business world.

When I left, former permanent secretary Ngiam Tong Dow told me: "You've never been a civil servant." I agree, though there is nothing wrong with being one.

The civil service gave me a lot of values, such as integrity, discipline and respect for law and order. You learn to be systematic and administratively correct so you do not have situations where records are missing or end up with deals that are shady.

A lot of people think civil servants can't be good businessmen, but I roundly refute that. To all the above, just add entrepreneurship.

Senior civil servants have a lot of plus points. Being familiar with rules and regulations and having gone through the big machinery of government, they fit in well with public-listed companies.

Many of these large companies are even more bureaucratic than the civil service and have even thicker instruction manuals.

Q: When you first took over Pidemco Land in 1996 and took a few years to venture overseas, people said: "Typical, humming and hawing and studying all reports like a bureaucrat." Why are you glad you took your time?

A: Surefootedness cannot be interpreted as being bureaucratic. It just means doing due diligence.

Before the Asian crisis in 1997, everyone talked about a second wing. Almost every property player went to Malaysia, Indonesia, Thailand, Hong Kong and the Philippines. They came to see me with huge artists' impressions of 1,000-hectare (10 sq km) townships they were building.

But I'm glad we examined ourselves and did not follow them. They were looking at things from a supply perspective, without studying demand. Sure, you can build it but who's going to buy? No one could answer me.

Would you consider that being bureaucratic or sensible?

So we don't believe in parachuting into a foreign country and developing a project. We want to be much more surefooted. We started out in Shanghai, then moved on to Beijing and now Guangzhou. When we start out in a new place, we post a chap there to acclimatise himself for a year. He literally lives as a Cantonese, doing nothing but recceing the place, meeting people, until he knows more than the officials do. Our return is his knowledge of the city and local operations.

That is how we have done it. Today, we operate in 78 cities. Now we've gained momentum, we can go faster.

Q: In internationalising CapitaLand at this bruising pace, what has been your toughest challenge?

A: Finding the right people to send overseas and making sure they have the cultural intelligence and affinity for the city they are operating in.

I've learnt a lot from watching other multinationals do it. For example, for a first posting, Japanese companies usually send their people to more neutral, easy-to-assimilate cities like Singapore and Sydney, before sending them on to New York, Paris or London.

Singapore, in particular, is a popular "deculturalisation" city for them to learn English, understand Western culture and orientate themselves. Then, after they finish their tour of duty after 15 to 20 years in the West, they are rewarded again with a short stint in Singapore, where they can play golf, eat Chinese food and feel comfortable, before they go back to Japan to become president or senior vice-president.

The other extreme is the American model, which tends to be less successful because MNCs throw them into the deep end, without much preparation. Sometimes, they appear too confrontational, brash and transactional, especially in Asia, because the distance between them and the culture they are operating in is too far.

Q: Your policy is to send only your best performers overseas. Why?

A: Yes, we always send A-graders. We don't send B- or C-graders because this is not an exile exercise.

Besides having competence and integrity, you must trust them, because they are operating thousands of miles away and creating a miniature CapitaLand.

A lot of companies make the mistake of sending someone who is not good enough. Others prefer to keep A-graders at home and recruit from outside.

Big mistake. Even if you hire an outsider who already has a good network and proven record of success in China, they won't understand your products, services, corporate value systems and idiosyncrasies.

That is why we always choose a promising insider who has spent a few years working with us. After a stint overseas, they come back to a good position. Everyone knows that whoever wants to take over my job as CEO has to have worked overseas for a minimum of three years.

Q: What about the other common areas companies often flounder in in their internationalisation efforts? How have you avoided them?

A: Many global companies just want to find a cheap place for production, but retain their command and control back in London, Tokyo, Paris, New York or Sydney.

But we run our overseas outfits like multi-local operations, instead of globalising outwards from Singapore. They have their own command and control and operate like local companies, with their own board of local directors.

But when in Japan, we behave like the Japanese, in Australia, like the Australians and in China, like the Chinese. But, of course, we retain our Singaporean value systems, such as no bribing.

Q: Singaporeans' inability to grease palms is often seen as a big disadvantage, especially when operating in developing countries. How does CapitaLand get around it?

A: Our typical project size in China is RMB2 billion to RMB3 billion, yet we don't pay a single yuan of bribe. Our principle is: If we have to bribe, we won't do business.

But you can establish a relationship with your country

host in a personal, helpful way, without the contamination of bribery.

Two years ago, the wife of one of our partners in China died but he dared not tell his daughter, who was then studying in Cornell University in the United States. Every time she called back asking for her mother, he lied that the latter had just stepped out.

We felt things could not go on like this and took the heartfelt initiative to help him, since he had never travelled out of China and could not speak English. We made the arrangements and sent someone along with him to the US to help him get through immigration, check into a hotel, break the news to his daughter, then bring him back to China.

Another example is when we built the Sheraton Hotel in Suzhou, we organised and financed a week-long trip to Europe for our partners from the Chinese tourism board to see how Sheraton hotels operate there.

As a consequence, our partners travelled with us, learnt with us, and ended up better educated on international practices. During the trip, they also became our friends.

If our partners sometimes need a space for a cultural art exhibition in one of our hotels, we don't charge them. If they have difficulty getting a visa in Singapore, we help them.

If they have children who just graduated from top universities, we can employ them. We have plenty of opportunities for such talent.

But if they want money, we say "No".

Q: What's your ultimate dream, besides seeing your masthead across every major city's skyline?

A: Besides that, my goal is to have more than 75% of revenue coming from overseas, even though we are in the very local and old business of property development.

In this business of building homes, offices and malls, we deal with all stratas of society—the rich, famous, eccentric and the masses. How many sectors have such impact?

So we want to show we are a lasting, reputable brand that builds iconic symbols of Singapore Inc. Right now, our Raffles City Shanghai mall is the best advertisement that Singapore can have.

Q: CapitaLand has moved upmarket from its unglamorous days of building utilitarian government projects to, these days, luxury projects like The Loft. How did you make-over the brand?

A: By being very detailed. I still review and approve every building's design. Sometimes, I throw some out. I make sure the people managing our projects are very hands-on.

The problem with Singaporeans is, after some time, they think they are big managers and delegate. Many get promoted too fast and don't spend time on the job getting to know the details. As they go higher, they know more and more, yet less and less. They generalise.

But if you don't understand detail, you can never build a brand.

A brand promises quality—which means artistry, function and reliability, within costs. In building a condominium project, I make sure buyers get the best value for their money. If the budget allows for it, I'll ask my designer to change to high-end German kitchen equipment.

We don't *tou gong jian liao* (偷工减料 cut corners in Mandarin). We pay our contractors on time and don't squeeze them. We also don't do open tenders but pre-qualify a panel of good quality contractors and negotiate prices with them.

We have a long-term relationship with them so they dare not cheat us.

Q: So you don't subscribe to the government's practice of open tendering?

A: No, it's not a clever model. The problem with tendering is that contractors choose you, you don't choose them.

Why? Because if they tender cheap, they will get your contract.

But I want to choose them. So I don't do bidding.

When I first came to this company, I was horrified that it asked for bids from engineers, lawyers and architects. I stopped it and started inviting proposals from the good ones we want to work with, then settling costs with them.

I was a contractor before so I know the costs and can't be bluffed.

Q: In time, what do you want people to associate CapitaLand with?

A: That we are very difficult people!
If we are buying services from you, we're very tough and drive a hard bargain. But if we sell to you, we'll give you the best.

Media Interview 2

Transforming A Brick-and-Mortar Company

The following interview took place in December 2006 as part of CNBC's Managing Asia *series.*

As the property market in Asia picks up, many developers are looking to scale new heights. One Singapore-based firm has gone so far as to transform itself from a conventional brick-and-mortar company to a new-economy player. Today, we get to meet the man at the helm of property giant CapitaLand.

Liew Mun Leong is behind CapitaLand's makeover. Within six years, he's modernised the Singapore-focused property company into an innovative, asset-light real estate player. The property veteran has been in charge since 2000, when government-linked firms Pidemco Land and DBS Land merged. Liew recalls the early days of reconciling the two diverse cultures.

"One is more, I would say, conservative and one is more maverick. And I think we today have a good blend on both sides now. Those issues are all over."

Over the years Liew has also divested some of his businesses, including one of his crown jewels, the iconic Raffles Hotel in Singapore.

"The starting point of the company is that you do have some very burdensome assets, assets that are very low-yield, and for us to improve our total returns, we'll have to transform them into higher-yield assets. Certainly there were emotions involved. Some of the hotels for example, not even Raffles, it hurt me a lot when I had to divest the Sheraton Hotel in Suzhou, which I personally built, but we cannot be emotional about it. We have to recognise that the shareholders are not going to reward you for your emotions. And you cannot return shareholders with emotions either. They did not invest emotions with you. They look for dividends, returns.

At the same time, CapitaLand has ramped up its expansion abroad, building everything from malls to serviced apartments in countries like Australia, Hong Kong, China and Japan.

"I must say there was a lot of pessimism about us exporting our capabilities. The analysts and the press would say nobody makes money out of exporting real estate simply because real estate is a very localized business. But we sat down and said we've no choice."

Today, over 80% of revenue comes from overseas. Total revenue has also grown to S$2.4 billion (US$1.54 million). Much of the credit goes to CEO Liew Mun Leong.

"Today we have to be more entrepreneurial, as illustrated by our overseas programme. We are a bit bolder than five years ago and because of being more successful, we're able to attract a wider diversity of people to the company."

Liew is also a pioneer of Asian real estate investment trusts, widely known as REITs. A REIT allows the public to invest into property without the hassle of physically buying into bricks and mortar.

"For CapitaLand, it's a way of generating more funds and income. We recognise that our balance sheet has been very burdensome, with low-yield returns. We saw in Asia a trend that increasingly we have to separate ownership and funding with the business itself. If you look at the West, a real estate company has investors and developers as separate parties. Increasingly, we found that funding will not just be from owner-managers. It may also come from banks like before. We saw the trend that we have to source for alternative ways of borrowing and financing real estate. In other words, we have to institutionalise the industry. So we saw REITs as a very good vehicle."

But Liew didn't strike gold the first time. I understand it wasn't easy when you made the first attempt to launch a REIT and it failed. What happened? What went wrong?

"REITs were a very new instrument. We were not experienced to identify the return. And we went for 6%. I realised this was not adequate because it was new. First, we pushed up the dividend to 7%. The logo was a big 7%. Second, we went on roadshows. We really educated the market, to talk about what REITs were all about. With the high dividend payout, better education, and a more concerted effort in structuring the deal and doing good roadshows, we succeeded the second time."

You were successful the following year with CapitaMall Trust in 2002. Did you have to work very hard to get the market to accept the product?

"Yes, certainly. We identified the best quality in our best shopping mall assets. In terms of shopping mall quality, they are the best. Then we put in creative people who understand how to build up the yield and how to build up a very certain growth story. What makes a REIT successful today, besides the quality of the assets, is you've got to have a very good growth story. Otherwise, it will be a bond. You're talking about 6% for many years, it'll behave like a bond and it will not have the capital appreciation."

Is it hard to find a growth story?

"No. If a real estate company like us develops a REIT, we can develop a stronger growth story. Take for example the concept in Junction 8, where we said, 'Look, Junction 8 has got malls and offices. The offices are giving us low yield of 2-3%. And the malls are giving a yield of 8-9%'. So what do we do? We mothball the plot ratio of the offices and allow us the additional plot ratio to build malls on the ground floor, which can command S$25 psf rent when offices are giving S$3. We went to the government and said, 'Look, we want to change the whole complexion of the asset from office to malls'. We call this decantation. Those are quite creative ideas. We are very fortunate that our people can think of that."

Was it easy to get government approval initially?

"No, because the government is quite stern about changing your usage. They will ask you why are you changing. When you tell them it is commercially more viable then they'll say you planned it wrongly in the first place. We say, yes, we've planned it wrongly. But slowly, they'll understand the story that for promoting REITs and to make the assets more productive *per se*, you have to accept changes."

How many REITs would you typically want to list altogether?

"We now have four. As soon as we have assets that are high-yield, we want to institutionalise them, to liquefy them; we'll do that because it is clearly more value creating. Just look at the Ascott REIT. Essentially, we're just taking a number of buildings in Singapore, China and Vietnam and put them into the REIT. Now, nothing has changed in the properties. But by doing that, we created more than S$400 million of value just out of this new financial instrument. At the same time, surprisingly, the mother share went up. The total picture is that if you have assets that can be 'REITed', we'll do it."

How many assets?

"We have assets all over the world. But I can say maybe eventually, we want to do 10 REITs."

You tell me 80% of revenue last year came from overseas. Mostly from Australia and China. What are you doing to diversify? Which areas are you counting on?

"We like to have 80% of earnings overseas. But this should not be taken as a rigid number, meaning, it's good to have a lot overseas. For example, over the last six months, Singapore started to grow. Real estate in Singapore is doing well. We will not cap it, just to stick to a number. That's something fundamental. We like to have a lot of earnings overseas to balance. At the same time, we're looking at other markets."

Such as?

"You see, we're now in GCC (Gulf Co-operation Council)—Abu Dhabi, Bahrain, we're building a huge project in Bahrain with other investors. In GCC we're looking at countries or cities that we're more comfortable with in terms of growth. Real growth, in terms of real demand, not speculative demand.

We are beginning to explore Russia, I mean two cities, Moscow and St Petersburg."

Today, CapitaLand is one of the contenders vying to build Singapore's second integrated casino resort. You're one of the bidders together with Kerzner International for the second integrated resort located at Sentosa. You lost out on the first one in Marina Bay. What are you doing this time round to increase your chances of winning the bid?

"In the first place, we now focus very much on the customers. What they need and also what they want. In the first time with Marina Bay, we concentrated on what they need but we neglected what they want. Now, it is a different story in Sentosa. We studied very carefully Singapore Tourism Board's strategy for 2015, the elements of tourism that they are eyeing. We examine them and more than that, we hit hard not just on the concept, also the design. So we appointed one of the world-famous architects, Frank Gehry, to design it."

How confident are you of winning this time?

"This time we really want to win. We have the best architect, the best entertainer, the best F&B and all that. All I can say is that we put in the effort."

What's your gut feel? Do you think you'll get it?

"I would be very disappointed if we don't win. I am very confident, looking at the competitors."

This will be your first foray in entertainment resorts. What are you doing to build up this area?

"Gone through first round with MGM. Now with Kerzner. We've a fair idea of what the entertainment, leisure and convention business is all about. We are now hopeful that we can secure Sentosa. Even if we don't, we could build up our capabilities in this sector, what I call the integrated leisure, entertainment and conventions business. And I think our partners, whether MGM or Kerzner, will still be with us if we have other ventures overseas."

In the last few years, outside of Singapore, you've invested heavily in China. It's one of your biggest markets. You recently announced that you'll expand into central China. What's you philosophy on what to invest and build in China?

"If you go back, for the last 12 years we've been in major gateway cities of Shanghai, then we moved north to Beijing and later, south to Guangzhou in the last three years. We've been very established in these cities. We feel that we should now move into a different market by way of geography. In the inner cities, the second- and third-tier cities, there is enormous demand for real estate, particularly housing. And we've found two good partners in two provinces, one in Chengdu, Sichuan and one in Henan. We're collaborating with them to build affordable quality housing in these cities."

How easy is it to find a good reliable partner in China?

"In the first place, you don't jump into bed with them immediately after you meet them. We have to do a lot of personal interaction and due diligence. For example, for the partnership in Chengdu and Henan, we met them, we had months of discussions with them. We talked to locals, we talked to others, to the government officials. We try to get the vibes on how the government views them as a local developer and then when we're ready, we go through due diligence more formally. After about six months, we were ready."

There is a lot of concern about exposure in China, given the recent policies by the government to curb overseas investment in the property sector. Do you see any dramatic slowdown?

"In the first place, let me set the stage right. In China, we are not just in residential. Residential is roughly one third of our business. We have more than 30 malls in China. Serviced apartments are a very big business for us. So are offices and mixed developments. Our pie is very balanced. Number two, I think in China, what the government does is to stabilise the market for the long-term interest of the real estate industry; they are good for us and we'll work with them. As it turns out, after a few months after the new measures, in fact prices have gone up. It does not affect us so much because in the first instance the measure is to curb foreign speculators; 95% of our business is to cater to the local Chinese, I'm quite happy with the progress with the new measures because it weeds out the not-so-strong or financially weak developers."

I understand retail malls are your fastest-growing segment. You recently launched two property funds to acquire assets in China and you've added on a China retail REIT this year. What's your retail strategy? What formula?

"There are two strategic issues. One is that we will build malls provided we can fill them. It's no point building beautiful malls when you can't fill them. So our main strategy is to link with a very strong retailer—Wal-Mart—they have got ambition. Wal-Mart will be able to fill up 40–50% of the mall and the rest we will open up to other retailers. So getting retailers is very important. Even in India, we went with Pantaloon—one of the strongest retailers there. Our strategy is not to go blindly to just build malls. If we can't fill them up, no deal. We look at location very critically. To that extent, Wal-Mart is very good. They do very detailed analysis of location for their malls."

You have the first-mover advantage, but the retail market in China is getting very competitive. Big real estate players like Simon Property, JPMorgan, all want to build more malls in China. How do you continue to get the best deals in China?

"In the retail mall business in China, we now have a good track record in terms of understanding the market. We won 21 malls with Wal-Mart simply because it has a lot of trust in us. We built Raffles City Shanghai and it was voted as the best mall in China in a public survey. We're known to be very good not in just building malls, but how to manage it, how to lease. We have good retailers. I think if you're just a financial group and you want to invest in malls, who will build them for you, who lease them for you? Who will manage the malls you? I think that's where our strength is."

In the last few years, you have been busy acquiring stakes in companies like Lai Fung and Central China Holdings. What else are you looking to acquire?

"That is the next wave of our growth. It's very arduous to acquire asset by asset. In the post-Asian crisis period, it's easy because nobody wants to touch assets. But that's during bad times. But during good times, acquiring assets is very difficult. So we think that one better way for growth is M&A. The idea is to have an early position into their business. And hopefully in two to three years, they go for IPO, that's our end game."

So you become a private equity investor in the meantime?

"To some extent, yes."

Any interest in acquiring companies closer to home, like Keppel Land and Mapletree?

"I think Singapore is very saturated in terms of number of players. In the first instance, six years ago, I said I must get out and I don't see how we should be more entrenched in this saturated market. It will be a very different strategy to think through if we want to grow larger in Singapore, especially if it is more domestic in its business earnings."

Is that an affirmative "No"?

"It is not an affirmative 'No'. Unless something comes up very attractive, I'll be very hesitant."

Mr Liew is a former civil servant turned property heavyweight. Liew has been credited with cementing his company's position as a leading real estate developer. You are trained as civil engineer. Do engineers make good businessmen?

"Engineers are very numeric. Very quantitative in their approach. To some extent we are quite cool and calculating. But that may be a disadvantage, having said that. But in terms of being analytical, numeric, logical, that's not enough. To be analytical and local is necessary, but insufficient to be a good businessman."

What does it take to be good CEO?

"I typically would coach my colleagues who are aspiring CEOs that they must have a strong vision. If you don't have a strong vision, no one will follow you. Secondly, I think the CEO needs to be interested in people. Not just lip service. The third is the courage to act. The inner self to act. If you have no conviction, it's not going to work."

You are 60-years-old and you've spent two decades in the construction industry. Has your management style evolved?

"As an engineer, it is still the same—being practical, eyeballing the project, going to construction sites, meeting with architects and builders. These are all standard things that I still enjoy very much. That's part of my work, although that cannot be a major part of my work now. So in terms of having operational feel, I'm still very much involved. That has not changed."

The last time I spoke to you, you told me you believed in the 3Ps—paranoia, perfection and perseverance has anything changed?

"The same mantra has guided us successfully. We're still very paranoid. We said we're going into Russia. We're very paranoid about what's going to happen there. There's still a sense of being guarded. We still want to be a perfectionist. We go to very detailed extent of how to do our projects. In terms of perseverance, we continue to persevere. If you look back when we first started a company, we couldn't have chosen a worse period. We went into turbulence, dot-com bust, 9/11 in New York, Iraq war, Bali bombing, SARS. It was a regular dose of crisis to the company, so we learnt that we need to persevere."

What's your ultimate ambition for CapitaLand, what sort of legacy do you want to leave behind?

"We certainly want to build an international and prosperous, lasting real estate company, a powerhouse in real estate in Asia Pacific. Today, we're number seven in Asia. If we can be in the top three to five, we'll be very happy about it. But being prosperous and international is not enough. My own personal vision, which my colleagues share, is to make it into a lasting company because it's much greater in achievement than just a prosperous company. That's our ambition."

Media Interview 3

Conversations With A CEO

This interview was conducted by Channel NewsAsia on 15 March 2007, as part of its Conversation With... *series. The 10-part programme engaged some of Asia's top political and business leaders in an indepth, one-on-one conversation.*

Liew Mun Leong (LML): Frogs are amphibians that have got 200 million years of history, older than mountains, which means they are really lasting animals. A frog is also an animal that is very much a reflection of the environment because it is very sensitive to the environment, it is a barometer of the environment. In many civilisations or societies, it represents prosperity; it represents happiness, health and long-lasting life. So in our zeal, in CapitaLand, to build prosperous and lasting companies, the important thing is lasting.

Interviewer (I): Liew Mun Leong (LML) is president and CEO of CapitaLand, Southeast Asia's largest real estate development group and one of the most profitable. This is a man who really is an architect of the New Asia.

Narrator (N): The world is his playground—with more than 20 years of experience in construction and real estate, LML has transformed CapitaLand Group beyond a traditional bricks-and-mortar real estate company that focuses on retail malls, offices and residences. It is also building up financial services by securitising its assets. All in the name of becoming a global player.

LML: My father worked in a factory as a fitter and I aspired to be somebody who is in a way higher than him. I still remember one day he told me, "If you can work better on in life under a ceiling fan, I will be very satisfied". Meaning, if you can be a clerk, he would be very satisfied. I think today we work much better than under a ceiling fan.

I: Do you think he ever imagined that you would be what you are today?

LML: No, it's out of this world. My father could never have imagined where we are today; this is the era of transformation, of the people of my time, the sharp transformation of all of us into different types of lifestyles, different types of economy, different types of countries.

I: You have transformed CapitaLand. CapitaLand is the largest Southeast Asian real estate developer and you also recently entered into what they call the billion-dollar club. How did you do it?

LML: First and foremost, let me say that last year, we did not plan to make a billion dollars post-tax. It was not in our budget. It was not in our plan, but as it turned out, our strategy has worked. We operated well, we executed well, our investments over the years have borne fruits, and the market likes the new things that we are doing, REITs, private equity real estate funds. So our overall business boomed as a result of the confluence of all these factors. But if you ask me what it takes, I reflect on all this and I say that it is due to three conventional factors of success, the three M's: You need Money, you need Markets, the right markets, and you need Manpower. I would like to say a bit more, because in terms of making a billion dollars, you've probably got to do in my business $3–4 billion of revenue, and this means you need a large balance sheet and you need to manage that. The Singapore market is very small, very limited. So we decided that we need to go out of Singapore. We decided that we need to be an international company, going into emerging markets, for example. And lastly you need manpower, and by that I am referring to talent, people; people who can manage your investments.

I: Now I have to ask you this question because it is the one that every single Singaporean homeowner would ask: Do you think that the Singapore market will continue to boom?

LML: I think we are in the cycle of growth for real estate. Don't forget real estate has slumped in Asia for many years and in Singapore particularly, and is now going through a growth stage. The economy has been restructured and as long as the economy grows, demand for real estate will grow. From the demand point of view, I would say that we will still be very, very healthy, and from the pricing point of view, you are in a robust economy. So my forecast for the next few years is that the real estate market will still be very healthy.

N: Headquartered in Singapore, CapitaLand's reach is international, given its foothold in more than 20 countries. China and Vietnam may be key markets, but the company has investments as far-flung as Russia.

I: You have always been interested in China. Where do you see the development now?

LML: We started operations in Shanghai, moved up north to Beijing, and Guangzhou, and these three cities are doing absolutely well. In fact, we have spun off into satellite cities and we are moving into the inner cities. We have started operations in Chengdu and we also have another operation in Henan. For these two inner cities, our plan is to grow on affordable housing, mass housing. In these two cities we have 35,000 apartments to build for the mass population for the next five years, so that will be our main housing programme. In shopping malls, we are very extensive. We are the largest shopping mall owner and operator in China. We have to date 72 malls in the pipeline all over, up to Inner Mongolia. They are all doing very well, all performing beyond our forecasts because the Chinese domestic market for consumption is just growing. I mean, they are very under-shopped in terms of shopping malls, under-shopped meaning that they do not have enough shopping malls to cater for what we call organised trade. Do not forget that Chinese are now buying computers, cameras, etc, that they cannot buy on the streets, they need shopping malls. That is where our strategy comes in. For serviced apartments, there is a big demand for serviced apartments because of business travel I mean, you are a business traveller and you are staying in a city for two weeks, you do not want to stay in hotels. You want to stay in a serviced apartment which is a home. Today, we have almost 3,000 serviced apartments in China; we intend to grow up to 10,000 in 2010.

I: Now China has been a very strong element for you, but you also have businesses extending into other areas as well, like Vietnam.

LML: We go to places or economies where there is demand, and there is affluence, there is economic growth. Vietnam's a classic case. Eighty million people, good GDP growth, high, strong urbanisation. In other words, they start from a very low base. So we go to these economies where there is demand, there is growth, there is political stability, I can put money there.

I: You can be seen very much as a crystal-ball gazer. You read a country, you read what people are going to be interested in, what they are going to need. How do you do this?

LML: Before I start up operations or business in a country or city, like say Guangzhou, I will put a man there for one and a half, two years, he will represent me, he will live there, read the papers there, watch the TV, eat the food, go to the restaurants, and really understand what the people there want. If I were to go to Chengdu, I will do the same thing. If Chengdu people play *mahjong*, why do they play *mahjong*? If they like to drink tea, why do they like to drink tea? So we do a lot of on-the-ground research; if I rely on paper research, I am dead.

I: To the extent that I understand that you would even go to discos!

LML: Yah, we went to discos, restaurants, we went to the back alleys in Shanghai. I ate, for RMB10 (US$1.33), two bowls of noodles, a bit dodgy on the stomach but we tried that so that we can appreciate the forces that make Shanghai work.

I: You have also extended, to places which for an Asian, at least, may perhaps seem a little bit remote, like Moscow and St Petersburg. Why?

LML: I do not think we should just confine ourselves to a culture or society that we are familiar with; in the mid '90s, we went to London, and we built a very successful project at Canary Wharf. We built a Four Seasons hotel, we built 322 apartments, we have shops, we have restaurants. When we planned that project, the British thought we were mad, that Singaporeans were mad. In the mid '90s, developers in London would build 50 apartments, 100 apartments, but 322 apartments, with a Four Seasons hotel, six restaurants, mad. But we think we saw the demand. My chap stayed there for a while, for one and a half years, before we plunged into that project. Whether it is an alien culture or place, the question is how much homework you want to do. For example, in our planning for the properties, different cultures require different designs, I mean I used to laugh at the British, why they carpet the toilets, why do they have to have two taps, why don't they use a mixer? The Chinese like their apartments to be large but the Hongkongers are not familiar with that, as theirs are small, so we know that if you go to China, you build big apartments because they do not like small apartments, so we've got to orientate to their tastes. The Japanese like to separate their bathroom from their bedrooms, they do not like attached bathrooms, and you got to understand that. So I think there is really a question of understanding customer needs.

I: The way you talk now, seems to me that there is a very compelling, intuitive element to business thinking, a rational thinking, and yet, you have been quoted as saying that you do not believe that you can be a good real estate developer if you are emotional.

LML: When you build up a building, it's like you raise a child, you are very emotionally attached to it. I built a very nice hotel in Suzhou called the Sheraton Hotel, with Tang dynasty design; I was very, very involved with it because culturally, it is very interesting. Now, many developers tend to be emotional with what they have built because they are personally involved; sometimes these are buildings that they have inherited from their grandfather, or father. There is also an emotional element. My main point is that these emotions exist because you bring up the building personally, and you are attached to it for years. For a publicly listed company, however, you have to learn to de-link your emotion. My thinking is that when shareholders invest in CapitaLand, they don't invest in emotions, they invest their money, $X per share, and they expect dividends, they expect capital gain. What I have to return to them is financial returns, total shareholder returns, so my emphasis is whilst we can be professional in building a nice building, and be passionate about building it, we should not be passionate about owning it.

I: Has there been a particular property with which there was a little tug at the heart when you had to sell it?

LML: Many. As I said, Sheraton in Suzhou, I was so involved with it, selecting the tiles, selecting the timber, doing the foundation, very emotional, but eventually I had to sell it; Four Seasons in London Canary Wharf I was also very involved in details and design.

I: Do you think that this is something that differentiates you from many of the other Asian real estate developers?

LML: We are in actual fact very different from other developers. We have transformed a real estate company, which is typically a very old bricks-and-mortar business, into what I call a new-economy business. What does that mean? We have created what we call a complete value chain for a property business. We are an investor, developer, operator, manager and financial adviser, in a complete value-chain proposition. In the entire property sector, whether it is homes, in shopping malls or offices, we have the complete value-chain capabilities. This is unique. We are uniquely able to internationalise our business; most people do not believe you can export real estate because real estate is a local business. Six years ago when we formed CapitaLand, we said we should internationalise ourselves, go overseas. All the press and all the analysts wrote us down. They said you can't make money going overseas. We proved to them that we could.

I: Let me play the devil's advocate. Over the past years that you have been expanding, you have also been riding on one of the most impressive growth periods in Asia. Expansion has been very, very great, consumption has been going up, there has been tremendous amount of capital looking for a place to invest, looking for a place to go home to, so you have been running through a period which has been very favourable for real estate developers. Can you survive a downturn?

LML: I disagree first with your point that we went through a favourable phase; let me correct your impression. We formed the company end-2000, November 2000. Immediately after that, for the next four years, or three and a half years, we ran into the perfect storm. If you recall, we had 9/11, the Internet bubble burst, the Iraq war, two Bali bombings, we went through the worst period in the Japanese economy, the worst period in the Singapore economy. A confluence of negative factors bundling up against us from 2000 to 2004. We rode through that. So I would disagree that we just happened to be successful because the past two years were successful years. We did the right thing, made the right strategy during bad times. Our thesis is that, even if in bad times, we could manage the market and do good investments. One of the things is that we do not rely on asset trading alone; that is why we went into the intellectual property business, we went into REITs, we went into private equity real estate funds. We diversify our businesses into different geographies because, don't forget, different countries have different property clocks, different circles, so we manage the property clocks very critically. If China is good but it may come down in certain quarters then we start to invest in India, so we have this balancing effect.

N: Never one to rest on its laurels, CapitaLand teamed up with foreign partners when the opportunity to enter into the integrated resort business in Singapore arose. The company may have failed in its bids, but the experience enabled CapitaLand to set up its ILEC unit, integrated leisure, entertainment and conventions.

I: CapitaLand took a little knock when it didn't win any of the IR projects in Singapore.

LML: Large disappointment...

I: I was going to ask you, what was your first reaction when you heard that you did not win?

LML: Within the first half hour, when I knew the result, I walked to my room, sat in front of the computer and sent an email to all my staff to say that we did not win it. The important thing is that although it came as a big letdown emotionally, within one hour or so, we picked ourselves up to try again. I think that is part of our success, that is, to face failure.

I: If you were to do something different, if now with the benefit of 20/20 hindsight, would you have made a different bid?

LML: We were beaten by the fact that we misread the possible demand for conventions. The market study shows that we need only half a million square feet (46,451 sq m) of new convention space. We pitched on that, but the winner pitched on the future. Instead of half a million demand, they pitched on 1.5 million sq ft. They were very entrepreneurial about it and I think it won my respect for being able to bid at that level. I think we should be much more entrepreneurial in terms of not just calculating the demand from the pure analysis point of view. That is point one. Point two, in the second case, we lost because we lost to the grand old brand of Universal. Branding is so important that, no matter how good you are, if you are pitching yourself against a very strong known brand, then you better think how you are going to defeat that brand. So the two lessons I learnt are that we should be more entrepreneurial and we should look at branding more seriously.

I: You have not given up entirely on the idea of leisure and entertainment. You have got a unit that is investing in that and has now taken a stake in Macau. Can you tell me a little more about that?

LML: Although we lost the bids, the benefit is that we learnt that as a developer, we have all the basics of building and developing something, whether it's a home, office or shopping mall. But in the resort entertainment area, we lack that content. But working on the two bids in Singapore, we have learnt a lot from these people who can provide us the content, from MGM Grand, and from Kerzner. We think that we should not waste the new knowledge that we have now gained, and with the new partnerships and the new domain knowledge, we can go into Asia for this new business. Our thinking is that as Asia blossoms and with more wealth, there is huge demand for entertainment, leisure, resorts. That's our position. Macau is our first foray. We are looking at China, India, even Japan.

I: Is that going to be the same as what we see in the West or will it be different in Asia?

LML: I think it ought to be slightly different. The consumerism in the US is slightly different from Asia. Even with Walt Disney in Japan, it decided to have rice burgers and it decided it should have a slightly different type of modelling of the theme park. I imagine there should be slight modification to attract the Asians. I mean, if you want to attract the Chinese, for example, the Chinese love shopping. So when you do a theme park that has a lot of wonderful shopping; the parents can go shopping and the kids can go do their stuff. You need to cater for that.

I: Any fond projects you hold in your heart?

LML: There are many. In Hong Kong, we bought Furama Hotel, tore it down and built a new building called AIG Building and made a lot of good returns, won a lot of prizes. I tell you the best inspiration I had 10 years ago was the HDB's success in building homes for 80% of our population; that is why I idolise the late Lim Kim San[1]. He's the man who provided HDB homes to 80% of the people, and with proper homes, the heartlanders have been transformed into better-quality people; so I mapped out our company credo as "building for people to build for people". We build for people. A building is just a building, but in the process of living in a good building, our people are built.

I: Liew Mun Leong has built skyscrapers, shopping malls and condos in more than 90 cities all over the world and he still oversees all the projects with great detail, down to the colour of the tiles and taps. He's an impressive combination of a robustly down-to-earth and the big-picture architectural visionary.

End Note

1 The late Lim Kim San was the first Chairman of Housing and Development Board (HDB), and best known for his contributions in housing the population of Singapore in the 1960s. He held ministerial positions in various ministries from finance, education, defence to environment. He was Chairman of the Council of Presidential Advisors and had also chaired various boards such as Port of Singapore Authority (PSA), Singapore Press Holdings (SPH) and Monetary Authority of Singapore (MAS).